Fundraising and Zombies

Fundraising and Zombies:
A Guide to Charity Management

John Baguley

Matador
9 Priory Business Park,
Wistow Road, Kibworth Beauchamp,
Leicestershire. LE8 0RX
Tel: (+44) 116 279 2299
Fax: (+44) 116 279 2277
Email: books@troubador.co.uk
Web: www.troubador.co.uk/matador

ISBN 978 1788033 671

British Library Cataloguing in Publication Data.
A catalogue record for this book is available from the British Library.

Typeset in 12pt Bembo by Troubador Publishing Ltd, Leicester, UK
Printed and bound in the UK by 4edge Limited

Matador is an imprint of Troubador Publishing Ltd

This book is dedicated to zombies everywhere. Rise-up, become professional- you have nothing left to lose!

Contents

Introduction

Most charities are well run, effective and efficient organisations which undertake incredible work often against all odds. This book, however, highlights a serious problem that lurks within the sector and shows how it can be resolved.

Allow me to introduce my old friend Paul who has a well-paid position, as head of fundraising at a very venerable charity.

His pay had been pegged to the cost of living when the organisation had been booming under a charismatic leader some thirty years earlier. Indeed, his salary still equated to the income of a high-flyer in a growing concern. Paul had never flown high; indeed anything approaching take-off gave him vertigo. Oh how he loved the quiet life! Arriving in the office rather later than his staff he would slowly take off his coat and scarf and hang them carefully on a coat hanger behind his door. Once he had unpacked his lunch box and put it in its regular place in the fridge he was ready for the morning's slow shuffle through the office. This meant he turned down ideas, stifled innovation and avoided looking at any figures. It also meant he did not see the director who saw fundraising as an unnecessary evil. So Paul was able to avoid him quite easily.

"There are three sorts of fundraisers," Paul used to say, "those who understand the maths and those who don't. Heh heh…"

Most of the charity's income came from the government in the form of an annual grant. Occasional legacies arrived from supporters who had known the organisation in its glory days. This provided just enough additional income to keep the organisation breathing.

Paul's staff worked best when he wasn't there. They rarely suggested anything new as Paul's stock response was, "We tried that years ago; it didn't work." If eager staff quoted another organisation's success he would snort, "Fine for them. It would never work for us."

And so it went on, year after year, as the supporters grew older and the work became less and less relevant to the unfortunate beneficiaries. The members of the board were allowed to serve as long as they could sidle into the meetings. Occasionally they felt a rather vague unease but this was soon offset by a fine lunch. As far as they could recall this was just the way things had always been. The chair, a rather complacent and pompous man, met with the director before the board meetings to ensure everything went smoothly. Unsurprisingly it usually did.

Shortly before the last general election a concatenation of unusual events led to Paul being exposed as a zombie.

The incoming government cut the organisation's grant by 30% to help balance their books, a new trust fundraiser was appointed and the chair died from food poisoning.

The new trust officer was passionate about the cause and the organisation's possibilities to expand rapidly. Following a strong hint from his brother in the finance department, he had kept his passion well muted at the interview. His brother had noticed that the previous trust officer had written excellent applications to major funders for large sums. Sadly Paul had other ideas and his pessimism about the world meant he never actually signed and submitted them to the grant-making trusts.

The board, none of whom wanted to move up to become chair, took the surprising decision to appoint a young whippersnapper on an interim basis (he was the nephew of the treasurer and reputedly quite bright).

The trust officer and interim chair took to each other at once, forming an alliance with sundry staff. Suddenly the director himself moved on shortly before a new firm of auditors carried out a full audit. The chair asked the senior managers, namely Paul, the finance director and head of operations, to write three-year strategies and budgets for their departments. As pressure mounted it became clear to everyone that only effective fundraising could save their jobs. Work quickly ground to a halt as

CVs were buffed up and sickies taken to see recruitment agencies.

All eyes were on Paul to produce a new fundraising strategy and, true to form, nothing happened. His deadlines sauntered by, laughing. The chair fumed but he found no allies on the board for drastic action. Recruitment of the new director was dragging on and redundancies looked imminent. It was then that the new trust officer made a serious miscalculation and accused Paul of being dead on his feet citing the pile of unsigned applications.

Never tell a zombie he is dead. Paul, as near as is possible for the undead, sprang to life and went for the trust officer's jugular. Accusing him of a serious breach of discipline he sacked him on the spot. The trust officer took the case to court. The case took time. Redundancy notices were handed out and the organisation shrank. The chair moved and a friend of one of the other trustees took his place. Eventually, a new director was appointed by the board. Reputed to be a safe pair of hands, he allowed the dust to settle and the trust officer to leave with a large pay-off.

Paul continued with the illusion that he was functioning in the real world, and the remaining staff kept their somewhat diminished salaries. Paul is still there. Indeed, Paul will be there long after I have passed on. I don't think he can die – he is, after all, a zombie. Hard as they are to work with, zombies are often much harder to kill off.

Paul may still be a friend, though one I could not work with. He needs an effective manager with strong human resources skills and policies to help him either develop or find the right niche elsewhere. Managers who pay staff off instead of confronting problems are part of a wider zombie-management problem. But at least they are taking action, unlike the surprising number of managers who tolerate zombies across the non-profit sector. I guess they lack the killer instinct.

So if the life of Paul does not appeal, take a long hard look at yourself and ask yourself what you can do to avoid his path and to live a rewarding life. Is a truly satisfying life one where you transform your organisation and the lives of its beneficiaries? Or will you always hunger after that dream job but settle for a lot less? Fundraisers particularly are often well placed to transform organisations by bringing in a huge increase in funds. Sadly however they often lack the drive and ambition to make it happen.

For example, many of us will recognise the scenario where we go to a fundraising convention and pick up good ideas about improving our fundraising techniques. But how many of us have really looked for the way to *double* our income in, say, three years? And how many of us are prepared to argue and win the resources that are needed to drive such a programme forward? After all that, we have to define the things we should stop doing, which is much harder than starting the new, cool activities. And so we fall into a pattern of improving things here and there, stalked by the danger that we too might turn into zombies.

Enough of zombies! Let us be heroes. A hero is someone who transforms their organisation and moves up to face greater challenges. This route is open to us all and it is about ambition and the desire to really achieve something. Of course it is hard and it is not just about long hours or being the boss's new best friend forever (although they may well be part of it).

A hero is someone who takes delight in excelling and understands how this contributes to the organisation's growth and thus delivers much better service to its beneficiaries. Heroes are brave and stand up for themselves, their colleagues, their department and their organisation. They are prepared to fight those internal battles for the right strategies, policies and resources that mean their work will have the significance it deserves. But there are vampires to be overcome and zombies to kill along the way! Perhaps you are just not up to it; but if you are then there is no better time to start than today.

With this book I hope to show you how to be a superhero, tackling zombies at *whatever* level they exist in your organisation. As such, it is a book about management and governance rather than solely fundraising but it is grounded in my experience as a fundraiser. The lessons and guidance are applicable to anyone working in charities, social enterprises, commercial companies and government departments.

The ambition to make a real difference is yours and yours alone. Good luck!

John Baguley

Chair
International Fundraising Consultancy
www.groupifc.com

1 Zombies on the board

Board members donate their time and expertise to lead your organisation but that's not a reason to act unprofessionally.

Once I worked very closely with an organisation where the chair used his position to appoint the other board members and it soon began to feel as if it was his personal charity. I remember when I was giving a presentation to the board explaining exactly why their fundraising was failing and what they as trustees needed to do to reverse their steady fall in income. To my horror they barely reacted and then went on with business as usual. This lack of reaction to events and even new possibilities is typical of zombie boards. Their lack of analysis and reflection, as demonstrated by their weak decision-making, is often staggering. When trustees change from watchdogs to lapdogs the organisation can be in serious trouble.

One mark of the zombie board, written across its forehead in blood, is an indifference to finance, particularly income-generation. Falling funds are brushed under the table. It is the fault of the economy, or the last recession, that they lament. In fact they will seize upon just about anything rather than heed any signals that the organisation is not performing as it should. In today's competitive market we know, do we not, that excellent performance in the field and in the office is not an aspiration but a starting point in the competition for funds. Fortunately, with increased scrutiny of how trustees lead charities following the 2016 report on charitable fundraising methods, the days of dithering rather than deciding are under threat.

But let's get back to that organisation and its falling-income dilemma. The organisation was fine so long as they had a great director and the trustees took a fairly hands-off approach. However, as with most badly run organisations, the day of reckoning came when a new director was appointed, who was passionate about providing an excellent service to the beneficiaries. The new director felt the organisation had not moved with the times and had failed to realise that its residential homes were outmoded, and that services which were more appropriate, such as debt relief, were required.

At first the trustees reacted with the typical stifling zombie inertia to the director's suggestions. More information was required, they moaned. Why do we need to do this now and can we trust the figures? Determined not to make a decision they concluded, "Not yet, let's review the situation next year." Their preference was for rambling discussions about the colour of the new logo that the director had proposed.

However, the director did not let things rest and having become even more convinced of the merits of his new direction, embarked on a professional fact-finding process to evaluate his approach. He decided to consult the local support groups. If you have ever seen a board versus local group fight, you will know that this is as close to civil war as you can get without shots being fired. The local groups loved the new thinking. They worked closely with the beneficiaries and they knew it made sense.

It all came to a head just before the AGM as many of the long-standing local group members had discovered they were members of the charity. This meant that they were entitled to vote, which they did most effectively. They were delighted at the host of resolutions in support of the new direction as well as some new governance procedures. At first the trustees reacted by digging their heels in before the meeting, disallowing proposals, changing motions, even leaving a couple of key items off the consolidated agenda. The latter they were sure would neutralise the effect of many of the remaining changes. The chair was heard to mutter repeatedly, "This just won't do!" as if his disapproval alone rendered the motions invalid.

Lawyers were consulted. There was much leafing through the Mem & Arts (Memorandum and Articles of Association) that set out the procedures for the AGM. Talk of tactics prevailed at any meeting of trustees. Fortunately the standard procedures were quite clear about the conduct of the meeting. On the day, the local group majority prevailed and a new set of individuals was appointed to the board with a mandate to make changes.

At first, the old chair and trustees muttered about betrayal and the imminent collapse of civilisation. However, there was little they could do. One by one, they staggered off. The new trustees brought in a governance expert, established transparent procedures and in time introduced two beneficiaries to the board. Everyone felt vindicated when these two new board members confirmed the difference that the new programme was making to their lives. The director was charged with developing monitoring and evaluation procedures to ensure the work was measured and remained relevant, and the organisation was well on its way to being a centre of excellence.

Working with zombie boards is incredibly tough for charity staff – ignore the telltale signs and you will let down your beneficiaries *and* your donors.

Zombie boards are hard to tackle because of the odd position they hold in having a degree of authority over salaried posts (in practice often just the director). They may have selected themselves to serve on the board or have been elected by a group of inactive 'members' who are not knowledgeable or even concerned about the outcome. This gives such boards an autonomy that makes it hard for the professional staff, or other stakeholders, to deal with problems. Even bringing policies and practices up to date can be difficult if trustees don't or cannot do that for themselves. Outsiders may feel accountable for the board's performance without having the slightest authority to change it. Ultimately, it is the Charity Commission that has the authority to sanction boards but this is only exercised in very serious cases and boards that are merely ineffective may escape scrutiny.

The result of a zombie board that carries on unchecked can be a disaster, with critical media attention sapping income and employees initiating grievances against trustees. And all this may result in financial irregularities, either real or imagined (the latter being harder to disprove), with trustees being exposed to personal liability if the charity is unincorporated. Now that really does focus the mind!

In management boards, groupthink can be crippling and is sometimes due to a lack of proper governance procedures. One telltale sign is a failure to set up proper search and recruitment teams and person specs for new board members.

Boards are particularly susceptible to groupthink as it provides familiarity and stability. However, it also makes it difficult to bring about change. Worse still, new board members may look around and think there is no point in trying to improve matters and leave. They may become zombies themselves if their first meeting is stultifying and they do not have a particularly strong life force of their own.

Indeed, some people can make a deathly dull meeting worse with their pessimism and negativity, which has to be fought and overcome if the board is ever to regain its positive momentum and make things happen. Listen out for those who decree that, "Nothing can be done," or, "It will never work."

And why do trustees say, "In my day..."? My response is a tart, "This is your day and you are, hopefully, alive right now." Worryingly it is often another sign that the board member's mindset belongs back in their old boardroom days of eons ago.

Some trustees arrive as zombies and are selected for all the wrong reasons or for no reason at all other than they knew someone on the board already. Worse still is the situation where the chair is filling seats with people most likely to agree with them. What made them zombies may be lost in the mists and they are harder to save than it is to find an appropriate analogy that does not involve the herding of cats.

This is not to say that trustees who slump into a zombie state cannot be revived. Managed correctly they can fully return to productive life but this happy state is almost impossible unless the chair is on board and active. The proverbial fish rots away from the head down and the influence of a zombie chair is so destructive that it must be addressed as a first priority, regardless of what other board issues there are.

Another priority is a lack of a fixed term of office – such as the usual three years with the option of a second term – after which you really are off and no sneaking back! No fixed term is particularly pernicious as it often leads to a long-term chair dominating the proceedings as well as clear group views reducing the organisation to inertia even when times change – and we frequently live in changing times, do we not?

Sometimes zombie boards are so bad at their job that the Charity Commission is called upon to exercise its guardianship powers and close the organisation. This rarely happens and it is more likely for the Charity Commission to put in an interim chair whose job it would be to build up a new board. Even in fraud cases, as there is usually one individual involved, the chances are the organisation will continue to operate once the Charity Commission is assured there are safeguards in place. A lack of diligence may be signalled by a board that sleepwalks through meetings and keeps on shuffling the papers without a real decision from one year to the next. Beware if your board is comprised mainly of people with a passing interest in the cause and no professional expertise. Are they really the only people willing to serve?

As with the organisation earlier in the introduction, fundraising is sometimes seen not just as a necessary evil but even a rather unnecessary one! For some board members it is as if funds arrive by magic because they are deserved not because they are professionally sought. This is turn gives zombie board members free rein to pay very little attention to income streams for a very long time. For them, increased income or a loss of income is seen as the consequence of unassailable external forces rather than neglecting professional fundraising techniques.

In stark contrast is the near-mythical US model that encourages board members to take an active role in fundraising. They are famously tasked to 'give, get or get off'. The benefit is that when board members get involved in events they meet the organisation's beneficiaries and key supporters. They learn about the everyday reality for beneficiaries through presentations, field trips and discussions and although such activity may take up staff time and involve some expenditure it is worth it in return for engaged and informed board members. Signs of an active board include board outings and training days.

Given a zombie board and a zombie director, an organisation may stagger on almost indefinitely until financial collapse puts it out of its misery. The situation is especially prevalent when a charismatic founder passes on after long years of devoted service. Such founders are bright, driven and passionate people who sometimes cannot abide contradiction and argument. What is the result? They appoint 'yes' people as their lieutenants and partners. They leave behind a board poorly equipped to cope without them. And still worse, it turns out that significant funds come from the founder's contacts whose loyalty is to the founder, rather than the organisation itself. The founder's friends will be prone to feeling that the organisation has 'lost its way' if the founder's original path is not followed to the letter.

Courting such donors in post-founder years may fall to remaining acolytes on the board. The problem here is that they cannot be removed because of their perceived proximity to these funders. It is far better to give fundraisers the freedom to invest in raising new funding streams, and by so doing accept the possibility of losing some donors as the organisation begins to adapt to the times. An organisation I worked with recently sold its residential premises in the Midlands and sought new offices in the capital. It easily weathered the storm from those major donors who had given to the appeal for the old building and were unhappy about its sale, because the trustees allowed the director to invest in new fundraising streams and in bringing on board new very wealthy donors.

Zombie chairs

Zombie chairs of the board are in a category of their own, being highly influential, and can cause serious problems when making, or avoiding making, key policy decisions for an organisation. Once the undead slump into the top seat anything can happen. They can fire perfectly competent directors or force them to move on when they seek to bring about much-needed change: something that zombies always find threatening. A zombie chair can eat the soul of the board, with good trustees moving on and half-dead ones remaining in post so that bizarre decisions sometimes become routine and staff feel unhinged by the reality with which they are confronted. Surprisingly, staff can often keep an organisation up and running quite effectively with a half-mad board for a long time even managing to shield beneficiaries from the effects of board decisions. Often it falls to funders, especially foundations and wealthy individuals, to scrutinise accounts before things change. And once these funders start to take a close interest in governance issues and staff morale, their questions increase and their donations decrease, and can cease altogether.

Understanding zombie chairs

To understand zombie chairs requires thought about the culture of their generation. By the time someone has become a chair they are often of mature years and will have served as trustee a few times before. Or perhaps they are recently retired from a commercial organisation. As the chair they will expect to be respected for their position, their time commitment as well as their skills acquired over many years of work. Today unfortunately none of this commands automatic respect and a combination of age-related bumbling, a lack of digital skills and zero respect drives them to fight a rearguard action against successive new ideas. Most retired business leaders are men and have often spent their lives surrounded by a team largely composed of other men. So when they sit on a charity board they feel at home, and disinclined at this time in their lives to turn things upside down by appointing women, disabled people, people from ethnic minorities or beneficiaries to the board. They cannot quite see why they should although they may not say as much aloud. It is precisely this mismatch between their thought and what they say that makes it hard to penetrate their facade of seemingly respectful behaviour. This gives zombie chairs their distinctive fuzzy outline. It is as if the real person, their soul if you will, is buried elsewhere or they are controlled by someone not present. If you know one you will understand exactly what I mean!

Good chairs

Good chairs will work with the director to ensure that they are ready and sufficiently trained to lead the organisation in new directions and to carry out vital new tasks. This can range from acquiring mission-critical new skills through to simply networking with new people who are vital for the organisation's development.

I talk here about the 'chair' but there is often a preference for 'chairman' and a loathing of 'chairperson'. I am not advocating for one in particular but noting that this is one point of entry where an interesting discussion may emerge with the person selected to serve.

Another sign of a good chair will be their attitude to their trustees, and their taking time to work with those who are struggling with, or resisting, new ideas. At board level, change is often fundamental. Not all board members will have the necessary skills to evaluate the journey that the organisation needs to take in order to fulfil its mission. Indeed, they may have joined the board specifically because they believed wholeheartedly in the old direction. This can lead to years of unhelpful behaviour and is best tackled head-on by an effective chair from the outset. This will prevent wasting everyone's time.

This can be a make-or-break time and board members who disagree with the new goals can be encouraged to leave and not to stay and fight. Unfortunately, the zombie tendency is to let it all wash over them with neither reaction nor enthusiasm. On occasion they do stagger into action and try to infect others with their misgivings. One sign it is time for these people to go is if they behave in this way *outside* of official meetings and in time become increasingly more toxic for the board and ultimately the organisation.

A good chair will try to find the skills that even a zombie trustee may possess and build on them (the trustee may never have been asked what they know, or what experience they bring from their daily life). A sensitive approach is better than 'head-on' as the trustee may well need to move on but a disgruntled trustee can do a lot of damage to an organisation's reputation.

Getting the best policies and practices

A key sign of an effective board is that, where possible, problems at board level are avoided or resolved thanks to strong governance structures, a positive culture and clear written policies and procedures.

It is important to remember that what is sometimes described as the culture of the board is really just bad practice that has ossified. When you hear, "We always do it this way," beware, as this behaviour can be hard to shift. Only through intensive and focussed discussion will the whole board concur that there are much better ways to proceed. This may come from comparisons with a range of similar organisations in a benchmarking exercise, or as a result of bringing in someone from outside the organisation who is an acknowledged expert: the *deus ex machina*. There are several excellent people and many consultancies that carry out this kind of work.

Even getting board members to attend on a regular basis is sometimes a chore and this can be simply resolved by an attendance policy whereby people are automatically off the board if they miss more than, say, two board meetings a year without good reason. Once people begin to attend regularly the chances are that their involvement and understanding of issues will improve and this will fuel a return to productive life.

Within the pile of policy documents a 'Conflict of Interest' statement is sometimes exceptionally useful. It undercuts one of the key problems that arises at board level where someone is pushing their personal or their company's agenda and they cannot or will not acknowledge that this is wrong, particularly if that was really why they came on the board in the first place. If the organisation is incorporated there are tight regulations in company law with regard to board directors and conflicts of interest, compliance being mandatory.

The chances of conflicts happening can be lessened by always having a few members form a search committee for new trustees equipped with a proper job description and person specification, which the whole board will have seen and approved. It is important to ensure that new trustees go through an induction process about the work of the organisation and their duties as a trustee. It is good if guidance, standing orders and policies are incorporated in a handbook, with a Code of Conduct for the trustees, so that people can refer to it to check if they feel things are not going as well as they should.

Should board members be expected to make financial donations to the organisation? Many give their skills, experience and time and these are as valuable as a large donation. They should be encouraged to give but the majority of board members simply don't. It does, however, help if they all give something occasionally to appeals like large capital appeals, because it significantly helps those appeals to say all the trustees have given, even if the sums are undisclosed.

Of course if the board members have been selected for their ability to give and their agreement to get, then that is a different matter, but they still need to deploy their talent (as well as wield a large bank balance). Once they have made a substantial donation they may well see this as their sole contribution. Some even feel it gives them a right to be pushy or unpleasant, as they have 'bought into the organisation' and should be able to dictate direction.

A key part of developing a board is to determine the length of time anyone may serve on the board and when they may reapply after their initial term in office. Nowadays it is usual for boards to work on three- or four-year terms with one reapplication. Even this approach means that groups of trustees can often serve for eight years, which is enough to bring out the zombie in anyone! Where relevant the chair can ensure that elections are held or alternatively the chair can ask those who are not pulling their weight to stand down rather than seek re-election. The latter is a collective responsibility of the whole board, even if it is the chair who actually carries out the deed.

Many UK charities have members who vote for some or all of the board members at the AGM. This group can be expanded as required to give a representative franchise. Some organisations have no clear idea of the identity of their members. In some instances their fundraising department has recruited supporters as voting members, which may entail a large AGM and a cumbersome voting process. For many organisations such as campaigning charities this may be essential to their ethos. For others it is a real hindrance and requires time spent revising the Mem & Arts perhaps with the Charity Commission to correct the situation and secure the most appropriate model.

Once the policies are set they need to be reviewed and renewed every few years (three to five is about right) to make sure they are driving the organisation in the correct direction. It is vital that the strategic vision remains relevant and is understood and followed. Naturally goals set as part of the organisation's strategy will change over time and the board should work closely with the director, with support from their senior staff, to set a new direction. Once the new goals are set, progress towards them has to be measured so that they can be monitored, otherwise they tend to become aspirations that are soon forgotten.

The time commitment that board members make should be explained and be included in their handbook. Though the actual time may vary it is very helpful for new members to know just what is expected of them. It is important too that they recognise just how much time they will spend working outside of board meetings. This means more than just reading the papers on the train on the way to the meetings! It means active participation on subcommittees, representing the organisation in society and participating in events as required and not just the celebrity events either. It may mean being a public speaker for the organisation. Though it will vary greatly from organisation to organisation, the time involved may amount to, say, five hours a month outside the main board meeting. This can be a huge and valuable asset for the organisation and properly run boards with committed trustees can help achieve the near-impossible.

Another significant question is: how much time should board members spend with staff? Sometimes, especially in the early years, board members and staff are barely distinguishable. However, as the organisation takes on paid workers the board should step back and become more concerned with policy rather than the practical. Of course, it is useful for both staff and board members to spend time together, and this may enrich their views and their decisions. It is often best if there are set times in the year when this is encouraged, but board members should refrain from meddling or micromanaging. It is much more productive to leave staff to undertake their own work.

On the other hand staff should not keep trustees in the dark and should have an open policy in regard to information that is not sensitive in either a personal or a business sense, e.g. if under the Data Protection Act the charity can hold relevant data on personal health which is germane to their work that may be restricted, or the charity may be helping people to become self-sufficient and that may be damaged by competitors knowing certain details so the information is restricted.

A special relationship

Change at board level and in the wider organisation can come from the chair working closely with the director to shape ideas for the overall organisational strategy. The director will then develop its details with the staff and present it to the board for approval. The importance of the relationship between the chair and the director is therefore vital and the morale of the entire organisation may rest upon it.

A really positive sign of an effective board is that the chair and the director review the talent the board needs and create job descriptions and person specifications for use by a newly established recruitment panel to find the talent that the board needs.

It is easier for the chair to instigate this than the director. By developing policy and practice and setting up some training they can search for new blood to inject into a lifeless body. The key policy is often limiting the years a board member can serve, but the drive to reinvigorate a board must not stop there. A zombie board will all too easily settle back into its old ways and infect new members much to the dismay of dedicated staff.

An enterprising director should first convince the chair that change is both desirable and necessary. The director may lack authority with trustees and will rely heavily on the force of the chair's personality to help effect positive change. It is sometimes a new director who realises the board is away with the fairies, and change is doubly hard at that stage because they have the additional problem of their probation to get through. In these early days they need to be seen to bring about serious change and this requires positive support from the board. This is of course the last thing on a zombie board's collective mind. Winning friends and influencing people is the answer. Only by engaging with each board member can a director hope the board will share their dreams for the future and agree the practical steps to move the organisation forward.

It is the role of the director to shape the path that the

organisation will take to achieve its mission and see its vision come to pass. This can be frustrated by a zombie chair who is not fully paying attention or is deliberately frustrating change. This situation can really test the mettle of the director. Can she handle the situation, manage upwards and get the other trustees behind her? Will she create the right momentum for the board that will lead to the election of a new chairperson?

Of course it can be dispiriting for a new director to realise that their first task is to sort out the board that has just hired them, but that is often exactly what the job demands.

Thankfully at some AGMs the board, once elected itself, elects all its officials such as the chair, secretary and treasurer, and this gives an annual opportunity to make serious adjustments, though that may take a few brave souls to carry out successfully. And the director need not take on the chair early in her time with the organisation.

If the director too loses her soul then the whole organisation is in dire straits. As a staff member I have seen a new director arrive confident and dynamic and full of great ideas that she discusses with her staff, honing them for presentation to the board. And what happened? Her confidence was gradually eroded as the board made revisions, failed to make a decision and ultimately turned down the much-needed new ideas. The organisation ended up with a watered-down version that made little difference. What a waste.

In my own time as a director I also experienced a board with its own agenda, which ran counter to that of the organisation but benefitted the egos and business interests of certain trustees. It was a bruising business as they lurched down their own wayward path, intelligent people unable to face up to the reality of their actions.

Managing upwards seems easy for some directors and a nightmare for others. But successful directors all have one thing in common and that is a trustee or group of trustees who will agree with them when they go in to bat on an important issue. Cultivating individual trustees and sounding them out about current issues is an invaluable exercise. It is very different from lobbying, which is often resented.

Having a friendly trustee give a positive message early in any debate has the power to swing a set of trustees behind a suggestion. Furthermore it gives trustees cover to disagree with the chair or a difficult fellow trustee. The trustee who speaks up first will be seen as taking any potential flak ensuring that those who agree with him are not left standing alone and exposed.

Enter the superhero

The answer to zombies on top is found when someone of great personal courage and organisational insight steps up and does what they think is morally right. Enter the superhero!

Superheroes are real people like you or me but they have qualities we sometimes lack, including a strong moral code coupled with a willingness to speak out even when there is little support for what they are saying. They are sometimes leaders-in-waiting or they may be actual leaders. Whichever it is, we come to respect them for the qualities that enable them to take a stand on key issues and articulate their case clearly. These are not barrack-room lawyers, whingers or toxic individuals, who are forever attacking the organisation. Instead they are people of principle who will fight the existence of zombies. They will work tirelessly to release zombies from their drug-like state and unearth instead a fully productive board member. And if that does not work they will ensure that the zombie leaves the organisation by mutual agreement.

Superheroes are neither shy nor retiring. They have a distinctive presence, speak at meetings and are obviously going places. They are often dressed for the next job level up and put in noticeable effort over and above their agreed hours. This is not merely wearing rather odd clothes to be noticed and staying late in the evening; it comes from a natural desire to hold a better position and being willing to put time into making things happen. Their networks are that much larger and more focussed on influential people than mine have ever been, and this gives them a subtle advantage sometimes enabling them to achieve things that look impossible at first. This advantage used to be the prerogative of the ruling classes, but today it is as often the built network of very effective people.

Charity Commission CC20

The Charity Commission publishes a very useful guide, numbered CC20, for the boards of fundraising charities, which all heroes should read in its entirety, and which is available on its website.

This is a quote from a section of CC20:

"Where, as is normal practice in many charities, you decide to delegate the day to day management of fundraising to your employees, you should have effective systems in place so that:

- delegation is clearly documented (for example in staff job descriptions, volunteers' role descriptions and committees' terms of reference) understood and implemented
- clear reporting procedures are in place, which include

    guidance on any particular matters that are to be
    reported to the trustees

- there are checks that the delegated authority is exercised properly
- you receive regular and fully documented report backs on agreed matters, presented in a way you can understand and use, and which allows you to exercise proper oversight."

In later chapters we will look at other characteristics of superheroes and see them in action against zombies and vampires. Vampires incidentally are those toxic folks who drain an organisation of its lifeblood by setting people against each other with a verve quite lacking in more passive zombies.

2 Zombie directors and zombie staff

Treading carefully here, I have an associate who once had a zombie boss and that was an experience she wasn't keen to repeat! Bright young creative meets shuffling depressive with a mean streak and a forty-cigs-a-day habit. "How are you?" was not a clever question and was usually met with a raised eyebrow and an unsaid, "Do you really want to know?" On a good day most suggestions were met with, "No, I don't think so," and on a bad day a puzzled expression passed across his face. He loved politics, seemed to read the papers all day and only spoke with real passion about what he had heard on *Newsnight.* He was not seen in the office anywhere near an election.

When I briefly worked there, it was impossible to have more than a brief word with him in the corridor as he came or went from meetings with 'important people' outside the office. It was these meetings he reported to the board and, thrilled with his closeness to people they had only ever seen on the television, they left him alone as if meeting people had become his job. Unfortunately, his ability to manage staff, develop an effective strategy or inspire anything beyond inertia was non-existent.

My associate had great ideas and ran her department with admirable efficiency but she soon had her therapist on speed dial. An unusually large government grant kept the organisation solvent. Its ability to deliver an effective service had long gone and its supporters and local group members were remarkable only for their age and dogmatic adherence to an institution that, like them, was long past its working life.

In this case no crisis came to the rescue and my associate moved on to escape the frustration, as had so many other clever and passionate people before her. They had all wanted to make a real difference but could not do so without support from above.

A zombie boss is bad, but a zombie head of another department can be just as alarming. I was running a rapidly expanding direct mail programme in the days when a five per cent return was not unrealistic – admittedly a long time ago – and budgeted to bring in 30,000 new members over the coming twelve months. It was great to meet the target and bring in more members in that year than ever before, but we soon ran into a problem when they started leaving in droves. It was only after a few months, when I ran a set of focus groups and surveys with lapsed but fairly new members, that the reason emerged. They were not hearing anything at all from us for months on end and they assumed the organisation was probably as hopelessly inefficient in its programme work as it was in dealing with its membership.

As I strolled into the relevant department to see who was responsible for membership fulfilment I saw to my horror that the desks were piled high with forms and the staff were struggling to get through the work. It turned out that, despite the budget, the zombie in charge had not bothered to hire additional staff to meet the anticipated workload, and had not bothered to bring in additional help when it was obvious that the staff could not cope. Fortunately, he solved that problem himself by retiring soon after but you cannot bank on that as zombies usually cling like limpets to their positions.

Is your boss a zombie?

Your boss may not be a terrible boss or that bad at his job, but he or she might just be there in person and not really there in spirit. A good boss sets out the work to be done, gives it a schedule and checks before it is complete that everything is as it should be. Once the task has been carried out he compliments you or helps you work out how to do it better next time. They are fair but firm. You wouldn't like to take them home, and they probably push you rather more than you would like, but you certainly learn from them. Looking back at a successful career, these are the people you will thank.

Such bosses also know approximately where they want their department to be in a few years' time, and they have an idea of the techniques that will be used and the staff and resources required to get there. In other words, they are leaders. A real leader inspires you to follow their vision of the future and unifies the organisation behind their goals.

A zombie department boss on the other hand lets you get on with it on your own, he doesn't say much until the results come in. If they are poor he accepts them as inevitable. On the other hand if you do well you won't hear from him at all. Zombie bosses have little idea about the future and so the same fundraising and other programmes take place in the same way year after depressing year. The organisation's CEO may set new targets for fundraising but they are rarely met and the zombie boss does not appear to be very bothered.

Their favourite phrases are: "I knew it would never work" and "We tried that a long time ago", with a few expressions like "I'll get back to you" thrown in. Of course they never do come back, find the figures or answer the question because they are not *really* there.

One characteristic of zombies is their inability to implement ideas. They may be great in a discussion putting counterarguments and even defending themselves in the staff room but actually putting an idea into practice seems to defeat them. Occasionally, as a consultant, I have had clients who greet each new idea with enthusiasm, share them around other departments, express gratitude for the insight and agree the actions to be taken before the next monthly meeting. And when that meeting comes around they will have done little apart from noting a minor problem or relaying what someone else has said. Actually carrying out the task will drift from month to month with no awareness that this time cannot be recovered. Especially in fundraising it is vital that techniques are put into practice in a timely manner, as the funds that could have been raised simply will not be recouped in subsequent months. When a full set of income streams is up and running there will be no slack in the system for delay or cancellation. Any delays mean that the money not raised will have gone elsewhere and however hard the organisation tries, it is unlikely to meet its budgeted income.

Sometimes bright staff just work round a zombie boss and organise things themselves, which is frustrating for them, but I have seen it working very well in the short term. Staff set their own objectives and organise things like the holidays and sickness records. Sometimes they lobby the boss's boss for the support they need and so long as they are discreet and do not let the zombie know he is not performing, it can be fun for a time. Inevitably, there will be times when the zombie asserts their position and stops or delays things. Sometimes the zombie's boss may even take the initiative and attempt to eliminate the zombie. This can work if the boss is a real superhero and understands how to employ the right human resources policies and practices. Sadly, however, the zombie often clings to his desk with a tenacity one can only admire and wish it were used to improve his work.

Dealing with a zombie boss

To deal with a senior zombie, our hero will need a dash of courage, patience and a clear understanding of employment law. Here, the trick is to know from the start that the zombie has to leave or be helped to improve, and that the latter may prove necessary but will take some time. Any hero must get backing for their actions as they may involve bloodshed and the courts, both of which are abhorrent to non-profit organisations and their boards. This is why zombies are often allowed to stay in post so long.

Forget offering them a step down or trying to park them in obscurity, that is mere cowardice, and the chances are that they won't go and you will just have set the organisation up for a charge of constructive dismissal. It is not that the zombie would win but perversely they may show a sudden animation in defending themselves. Perhaps the thought of being called back to the underworld because they have lost their job and their niche in our world is electrifying.

The only way to win is to be terribly nice, offer training where appropriate, set a series of targets (sometimes for everyone including the zombie) then watch the zombie fail to meet them. At this point do not be afraid of setting more targets until you have a clear case for dismissal or see a distinct improvement. Of course, if the zombie does turn nasty the hero can go for instant dismissal but be warned, you need proof and backup. Can't you just pay them some money to go? The answer is 'yes', but this is a process which needs proper legal advice. If there's a budget to do so it is possible and often more commercially palatable to offer a negotiated severance under which the zombie resigns and is paid some money under a settlement agreement (formerly 'compromise agreement'). Perversely the deeper the zombie state the more expensive striking a deal may turn out to be. A zombie will want money to cover his or her gap in earnings between leaving you and starting in a new role. Zombies tend to realise they will not be hot property on the job market so that gap for which they want compensating may be a long (and expensive) one. The 'without prejudice'/off the record approach to losing a zombie is full of bear traps so a few minutes on the phone to an employment lawyer or other qualified trusted advisor will pay dividends.

In all this, the last thing the hero should do is to merely annoy the zombie, or they might just spring temporarily to life and work plausibly well for a bit until the heat dies down.

Helping zombie staff

The situation for zombie staff who are not heads of department is really rather similar. Primarily, it is their boss who needs to take action and to do that as early as possible. Often newly appointed staff arrive with high hopes and great expectations but then they are left alone by their boss when pressing problems emerge and the serious process of their management is forgotten. It is also easy to leave bright newcomers to get on with their work without proper management, but this can also be demoralising as they may feel ignored. If their first actions are unobserved or go unremarked on they may feel that the results do not matter to their boss or to the organisation. If they feel this way they may as well just relax as no one cares. Psychologically this can undermine the best of us and lead to underachievement. More importantly it can allow the worst in us to come out and our love of the organisation's work that first inspired us can turn into cynicism. It may result in whingeing and complaints or become internalised by the individual and expressed through zombie-like behaviour.

Dismissing staff

In the UK no one has a secure position for the first two years of their employment and dismissal can be immediate, but it is a poor state of affairs if, having presumably survived a few months' probation, someone turns out not to be up to the job or turns into a zombie. That may well say more about the organisation's management skills than about the staff member in question.

The basis for dismissal after two years can be ability (can they actually carry out the job?), conduct (do they behave reasonably with other staff?), capability to do the work as a result of extraneous circumstances (like a lorry driver losing his licence), or redundancy (when the position no longer exists through lack of funds or strategic development). Managers sometimes shrink away from the legal means of dismissal because they must be fair and this is only the case if they act reasonably; but what is reasonable is not defined and so managers, who should be resolute, fear a court case for unfair dismissal. How afraid should they be? Well, the cost of an unfair dismissal is capped at law. Currently the compensatory award is the lower of: (a) the statutory cap (around £80,000) and (b) a year's pay. Things get much more expensive if the zombie can argue successfully at the Employment Tribunal that he or she was fired or subjected to detriments because of his or her disability, age, sex, race, sexual orientation, pregnancy, religion or belief (the 'protected characteristics'). Compensation for discrimination is not capped and will consist of an 'injury to feelings' award of up to £33,000 plus a compensation payment to reflect the financial loss suffered (in reality the gap between the termination date and the date the ex-employee finds a new role with pay parity).

Of course theft, fraud and violence can result in immediate dismissal whatever the length of service, without notice or pay in lieu of notice; but if you are investigating the matter you can only suspend the person without pay if their contract contains a clause to that effect.

Under current legislation it is harder than ever for employees to take employers to court in such cases as they must pay for it themselves rather than seek legal aid and even have to pay a court fee to get their claim heard and a hearing fee if it goes all the way to trial. Cases dropped by 80% following the introduction of fees in 2013. However, the ghost of tribunals past still lurks in the back of managers' minds. Contracts are indeed becoming tougher with clauses on instant dismissal without pay or notice, and when many jobs barely pay a living wage it is becoming less likely that those applying for posts will either scrutinise the small print or object to it. The even-handed nature of contracts that many of us knew so well is being squeezed out as they are handed to lawyers to revise into punitive one-sided agreements. The days of reasonable pay and fairly generous conditions to attract workers have long gone.

Naturally, no one should dismiss staff without a discussion with the Human Resources (HR) department or a company lawyer, but dismissal is only one way to deal with zombies and may not be the best. Though, whilst we are looking at dismissal, there are two other aspects that should be covered because they are rife in the sector.

The first is constructive dismissal and the UK government website says this happens when an employee resigns on the grounds that the terms of their employment contract have been broken. For example, if you as the employer:

- cut their wages without agreement
- unlawfully demote them (i.e. where you do not have the contractual right to do so)
- allow them to be harassed, bullied or discriminated against
- unfairly increase their workload
- change the location of their workplace at short notice or
- make them work in dangerous conditions

then you could be facing a claim for constructive dismissal. It's not a particularly attractive claim for the employee to bring: to win at the Tribunal he or she needs to demonstrate that there was indeed a 'repudiatory breach' (which only means a really serious one like those listed above). Not only that, the employee has to resign immediately in response to that breach. This means the employee does not work their notice so they essentially summarily dismiss themselves. The claim would be worth the money the employee would have received during their notice period and, if they have two years' continuous service, they can bring a claim for unfair dismissal.

It would be hard to show that a breach of contract was a fair thing to do and constructive dismissal can result in a claim for wrongful dismissal. Wrongful dismissal happens when an employee's contract is broken during the dismissal process.

If not dismissal…

Zombies are extreme cases but they can often be brought back from their half-life to become fully functioning humans, but only if they are truly willing. Giving them a second chance on the understanding that this is a real opportunity, not mere procrastination in firing them, can have surprising results. It is as if someone had called their bluff and they knew the game was up, but appreciated the chance to redeem themselves.

I am far less tolerant of zombie directors or trustees and I am especially intolerant of zombie chairs of the board.

These are senior positions and there is no excuse for bad behaviour and extremely poor performance. With rank and file staff I think much can be done and the fault often lies in large measure with the people to whom they report, who should have taken action long before they became zombies.

This is usually done on an individual basis, but in large organisations it may require a whole retraining programme. In 2014, IBM sent about a hundred staff a memo saying: "… some managers and employees have not kept pace with acquiring the skills and expertise needed to address changing client needs, technology and market requirements," and then, "You have been identified as one of these employees. The retraining will last six months with one day a week being devoted to learning and development."

The surprising sting in the tail was that for this time the wages of the one hundred staff were to be cut by 10% to pay for the training or what IBM called a "co-investment" in IBM's expense of training them.

While retraining can help zombies it is rarely enough on its own and there needs to be stick as well as carrot. The stick is usually performance targets that need to be met to show that they can meet the job requirements once they are given the chance and the right skills. Sometimes of course it is the mental attitude that needs to change and that may come from more individual attention and personal advice. This requires sensitivity and a degree of emotional intelligence that a manager should possess, but which may be sadly lacking; indeed the wrong kind of attention can amount to constructive dismissal if it amounts to bullying.

The best kind of manager may find that the problem lies with current systems or approaches that are ineffective. Chances are that the staff member in question knows this and has modified their behaviour and simply goes through the motions because no one is listening or really ensuring that sensible change happens. The lack of a mechanism for employee feedback, or just the fact a manager has not kept pace themselves with the rate of change in fundraising or management techniques, can result in loss of money and reputation in a very short space of time.

Creating the right environment

So far we have looked at individuals but they only exist (or semi-exist) in a context and that context can support and develop them or restrict and stifle them. The zombie in your midst may be an extreme reaction to their environment and that consists of the physical space (heating, lighting, and desk space), workplace traditions (coffee breaks, smoking breaks) and corporate practices (staff policies, rewards, and terms of service). But let's not forget the importance of their manager's attitude, expectations and behaviour. The most influential people in our lives are usually our partner and our boss. Together they have the capacity to make our lives heaven or hell plus all points in between.

Caring about your clients, customers or donors is obvious, but in civil society we tend not to care so well about our staff and there is still a hangover from the days when charity work was a job for wealthy benefactors epitomised by Lady Bountiful. This attitude comes with a belief that charity staff should all be volunteers or feel themselves very lucky to be paid at all let alone have 'perks' like pensions.

A professional attitude to running a non-profit will treat staff as valuable professionals to be retained in many of the same ways that effective companies retain their valued staff. In our sector, because our work has a strong moral basis in equality and fairness for all, we should be beacons of best practice. If we are not, perhaps we need to question whether our organisation is the right one to deliver its services.

Of course, professional non-profits are clear about the terms and conditions of employment: salary, pension, holidays, maternity leave etc. And it should not end there because the atmosphere at work from day to day is often as important as the package we buy into when we accept the job. This, perhaps more than anything, is why we stay or leave an organisation. Some of the factors that create that atmosphere include:

- how we celebrate success
- how we deal with failure
- how we communicate across the organisation
- how much our managers know and understand about us and our work
- whether we feel valued
- how the direction and goals of the organisation are communicated
- how our work relates to those goals
- how we relate to the staff around us.

While we may not be able to turn around a whole organisation overnight we can offer individuals who are exhibiting zombie tendencies some mentoring to help them develop. This is a more formal process than their manager paying close attention to them or their work, and is often carried out by an outsider because they have the skills that the zombie lacks and more importantly can communicate those skills effectively. The very act of mentoring provides a degree of close attention that will change behaviour and see a new attitude emerge. In return the staff member will be expected to improve their performance and this should be monitored in a measurable way.

Dealing with the disaffected

On the other hand a negative attitude and deep-rooted cynicism may be more than any mentor can shift, and if this is the problem then it is the mentor's duty to let management know they have a serious problem of disaffection. Changing someone's character may be beyond the remit of any organisation; however, if it interferes with either their work or the work of other staff then the organisation may not be able to retain them.

Later we'll look at toxic individuals who affect the performance of other staff and suck their lifeblood – these are of course the legendary vampires. This toxicity is a separate problem and one that is very hard to deal with among senior managers. As with other management issues it is solvable and requires attention whilst it is still a small problem and still containable.

Generation wars in the workplace

A failure to move with the times can induce a zombie state, rather like the time said to be spent underground by paralysed victims of Voodoo before they are resurrected as zombies. Cocooned in their own privileges, with a secretary to bring them printouts of emails, they miss the point of social media and become too slow to respond to changes in workplace practice to effectively compete with other organisations. This is especially true with the changes in fundraising as old print media becomes increasingly unresponsive and new online ideas prove increasingly effective. However, it also applies to communications, campaigning and swathes of our lives outside the workplace.

In addition, changing attitudes to conduct in the workplace can be the root cause of unproductive people and lead to unproductive departments. This is especially true as the pace of generational change speeds up with Generations X and Y working with Baby Boomer managers who are accustomed to a workplace where they were entitled to secretaries and are still waiting for the Internet to vanish so they can get back to hard-copy memos. That prized corner office no longer carries any distinction now that the office is open-plan – someone hot-desks in another corner and half the workforce is at home anyway. Today people have already discussed and agreed what will happen on social media before the old-fashioned boss has even entered the office in the morning.

A quick recap on the generations to help you flush out any zombie behaviour in your midst:

Baby Boomers were born between 1945 and 1965, which was a boom-time for births and also a time that saw enormous social change and a loosening of the pre-war deference to authority. This, combined with relatively affluent teenagers, created a large-scale demand for music, fashion and films, and proved to be an explosive mix.

Generation X (born 1966 to 1985) came of age during the Thatcher/Reagan era that denied the social function of government and created growth through a massive increase in personal debt and a 'loadsa money' or 'I'm alright Jack' attitude. 'Thatcher's children' were the latchkey Gen X kids brought up to be independent and self-sufficient, but who often reacted for a time by adopting the slacker culture of knowing but unengaged youth. Today they have built huge digital empires and are hands-on 'helicopter' parents.

Generation Y (born 1986 to 2006) were the first digital natives who see no point in coming offline to receive out-of-date news, comments or opinions. The years of Tony Blair's leadership left them sceptical of politics, comfortable with debt and afraid of global warming – blaming the Boomers for their social and economic problems. The crippling waves of austerity, under the UK's Coalition Government, only served to reinforce these prejudices.

Unfortunately, the passionate new Generation Y staff member can become quickly disillusioned as their innate use of mobile technology and social connectedness is discounted. They may even find restrictions on the use of some Internet tools, which they find at best ridiculous and at worst a confirmation that they have made the wrong decision in accepting the job offer.

With all three generational cohorts working in the same office their use of time may also become a source of conflict, with Boomers expecting staff to find work to do when a particular job is finished, and Generation X using the time between assignments as downtime. And then there's Generation Y using it to develop and explore their social networks, which Boomers may view as an irresponsible use of the working day.

Bringing any of these people back from zombie-status requires an understanding of their background and culture as well as a knowledge of the individual person, as we cannot apply generational characteristics to everyone in any one generation. Building a strong corporate culture in which everyone flourishes can mean that we communicate through multiple channels, accept some differences in behaviour and recognise there are multiple routes to the success of corporate or social goals.

Andy Grove of Intel has said that to remain competitive an organisation must change as rapidly as the change in its external environment. There is no doubt that we are living through unprecedented change which demands that our organisations, and by default our workforces, must be as flexible as possible in order to accommodate change and the current range of staff expectations. In time the Boomers will retire, though they are taking their time about it, often stretching their employment into what was once considered old age. New generations will take their place expecting to work in different ways based on society's evolution and its use of digital technology, and even technologies we do not yet know, which will make their presence felt soon enough.

A new brand of zombies

One key development for civil society is the emergence of social enterprises and the increasing amount of government funding available to them globally. Even without the tax advantages or support structures of traditional charities, they have rapidly attracted large numbers of young entrepreneurs and built their own support networks and structures. Remember Impact Hubs and how, in a very few years, they became a global phenomenon? Though social enterprises are there for social good they are also for-profit organisations and not voluntary in that the founders make money as well as helping people and the environment.

As yet social enterprises are probably too new to have acquired their own brand of zombies, and it remains to be seen if the for-profit drive will be enough for managers and founders to tackle them head-on in an effective manner. From what we know of conventional commercial enterprises they are better at tackling personnel problems but are very far from having solved them. Their scale and rate of growth can create backwaters that remain relatively hidden until a crisis occurs, and then both the slack and the slackers need to be removed from the system. When commercial enterprises or charities go under, the immediate cause may be market forces, cash flow or unforeseen dangers, but like the Co-operative Bank and the larger Co-op movement, the power of individual zombies to bring serious trouble should not be overlooked.

So what about Paul?

Those of you who have read the introduction to this book may recall the case of my friend Paul with whom I discussed using his experience as the basis for my first blog on zombies. So long as he wasn't identified he was happy, but of course he had the firm belief that in his case (he saw my blog as a typical piece of journalistic exaggeration) his actions were not only fully justified, but he had saved the organisation from the bankruptcy which an expansionist fundraising strategy would have brought about. In any case he said no one read blogs, especially about fundraising, or books on fundraising for that matter.

I asked him for his reaction to suggestions that he retrain in order to have the skills to help his department integrate their fundraising with the Internet and, for example, to link to their supporters by email, but he said that was a waste of money and he wasn't interested, and online fundraising was a temporary fad which sucked up huge amounts of staff time producing few real benefits. Paul's retirement is not far off and he is confident that he will get there whilst working for the same organisation. I too am confident that is what he will do!

I asked what would happen if he were to set targets to reach and he explained he already had targets, which were in the budget that he had himself set, and he had reached them so there was no problem. If someone gave him new unrealistic targets to try and get rid of him he would fight them and it would probably count as constructive dismissal. Also if someone gave him Internet-related courses to go on or instructions to set up online fundraising they would be wasting the charity's money and he would complain to the trustees.

Naturally, I find this stonewalling and refusal to move with the times rather distressing but it is a good example of how it may take a lot of determination to shift or develop individual zombies, particularly in organisations where the culture is not dynamic, expectations of staff are low and staff are prone to fight a management that does not lead with passion.

Changing cultures

In cases like this where the culture is weak and the organisation seems to have run out of steam it takes a top-down shift to shake things up and produce a new effective and efficient working practice. If the chair and board of trustees can set the forward strategy with the CEO and are prepared to back the CEO in carrying out organisational change then real progress is possible.

Benchmarking against other organisations (for example via FundRatios from the Institute of Fundraising) and acting on management concepts, such as those in the book by Jim Collins, *Good to Great*, can lead to realistic changes. This in turn leads to positive results and an organisation that improves year on year, delivering a better service to its beneficiaries and showing its donors that their money has been well spent.

Of course, cultural change takes a long time to effect but once accomplished it tends to stick if it is successful and staff can see the improvements and their role in those improvements. If children play games for two years in the playground those games tend to become part of that school's traditions lasting for many years; similarly if a policy, practice or corporate myth is repeated for two or three years it stands a good chance of surviving in the organisation's bloodstream for quite some time.

As a more dynamic regime takes hold it can also convert or shake out zombies who either finally feel inspired or see no place for themselves in the new system. This is not to say that one should restructure just to lose or convert zombies; indeed, that kind of change for objectives other than to make a more efficient and effective organisation can just set people against each other. What's more it runs the risk of failing to engage the required number of staff to guarantee success.

Success, dynamic change and a flexibility to take up new challenges do bring new risks. Any increased pace of working can induce burnout if not sensitively managed. When people put in extra effort to perform new tasks they require careful managing if they are not to turn against the change per se and retreat into a zombie-like shell. Increased success in the field of endeavour may also bring attention from rivals or the media at a time when the organisation may not be entirely prepared for such scrutiny and indeed may only be part way through changes it does not want publicly discussed until staff are fully committed.

The brand bandwagon

It may appear logical that, as these changes go through and achieving success is becoming part of the charity's culture, all ties with the old organisation are signalled by a change of brand to 'New Style Organisation'. And whilst that may indeed be appropriate in due course, rushing into a rebranding can provide the one thing that can unite everyone against change and become a symbol of resistance.

We have a lot psychologically invested in our work and who we work for, and whilst much change is internal, once the organisational brand changes, it may not epitomise quite what we have always felt about our work. The very act of selecting a new brand may feel a bit like selecting a new organisation for which to work. Added to this, we all feel that we know best when it comes to choosing logos and such like which means it is almost inevitable that there will be both winners and losers when the final brand choice is made. Losers are not great bedfellows during organisational change.

On the other hand, once the internal work is done and people have settled down into new working patterns then a change of branding may well cement this way of doing things for everyone.

Though this chapter often mentions fundraising it is

illustrative of management principles and techniques that apply equally well in the field of communication, policy, finance et al.

In the next chapter we'll look at a different kind of zombie. This zombie was never a human being yet it can live on long past its drop-by date: the zombie fundraising technique that should have been laid to rest long ago.

3   Hiring zombies - not

After reading the first three chapters you may be forgiven for thinking that the third sector is hopeless at recruitment and chock-full of zombies dragging it down! Of course, that is not the case and I have seen a steady increase in professionalism at all levels with excellent recruitment practices developing year by year. However there are still many organisations, especially (but not exclusively) the medium and small charities, where recruitment is undertaken by one person with little time or understanding of the process.

Considering the damage zombies can do and the critical importance of getting the right people on the bus, in the right place, recruitment is a task all effective managers need to be closely involved with throughout their careers.

One of my consultancy's early clients seemed to have cornered the market for zombies, from the person in reception who was always on the phone and gave the impression that visitors were a nuisance, to the head of finance who seemed to think he was head of fundraising too and there to prevent anything new happening. The head of fundraising himself seemed eternally weary of the whole organisation, and we would sit and discuss the practical steps he could take over afternoon tea until it was time to go home. We'd then begin again from square one at the following monthly meeting. After a while, I found myself starting to run the department as I brought other staff into our meetings and found that he would agree to almost anything I suggested, provided it didn't cost money, and they could then go ahead and carry it out.

The CEO, who had served with me on the board of another charity, had asked me to help and was very positive about this development, but it was hardly appropriate as I was slipping into a role I was used to fulfilling but which was not consultancy. Several staff members were calling me for the go-ahead on projects and others were complaining to me about the speed of change as if I really were in charge.

Whilst I was looking for a new strategy and seriously considering bringing the whole thing to a halt, the head of fundraising went on sick leave (signed off due to stress) and never came back. I was asked to help with recruitment, looked over the new job description (no one could find the old one) and attended the interviews with the CEO and one of the trustees. It immediately became apparent what was wrong. As I scored my copy of the chart I had drawn up for each of us against the candidates' answers I noticed that no one else was completing theirs. After the first couple of questions their charts just had doodles on them. At the end they both said, "We talked about this beforehand and we want Brian to get the job, because he worked at charity X," which was the leading charity in their field. Looking at my scores I could see they were missing out on some remarkable candidates and Brian had only been at X for about a year and a half which seemed to be his maximum time in any job. I asked for time to discuss the other candidates but they were not really listening, and whilst being patronising by complimenting me on the system, they were ignoring it. There may be many other ways of interviewing potential staff, and probably better approaches than the one I used, but choosing people on only one metric is highly dangerous.

Right forms, wrong behaviours

There are unfortunately other mistakes that can be easily made. When I worked at Amnesty, or was it at Friends of the Earth, or maybe at the Medical Foundation, I found that our new well-organised recruitment process wasn't working in the way it was intended. We had carefully written the fundraising job descriptions to fit on one side of A4: covering reporting relationships, a clear summary of the job and an agreed list of specific tasks. And of course there was the usual 'and anything else we ask you to do' get-out clause. Then we wrote a person specification which really showed the kind of person we wanted and listed how we would discover each characteristic from the interview, their CV or a test. Mostly though it came down to the interview. We set aside three-quarters of an hour for each interview with a fifteen-minute break between candidates and set of eight to ten questions (which related directly to the person spec) as well as a diversity question at the end.

All that tied the interview process together with a clear, explicable logic. However the problem was that I was faced with a set of people who answered all the questions quite well which meant we fell back on who we liked best which easily becomes 'people like us'. Of course we diversified the interview panel but I was not a happy bunny. Then I discovered how the zombies had slipped in. Despite opinions to the contrary, zombies can be quite cunning. The HR people were dutifully sending out the person specification with the job description, so given a modicum of astuteness, everyone could see the obvious lines of questioning and prepare themselves.

So, you ask, didn't we ask for references? Of course we did and what a sense of relief it was for employers to give a reference to a zombie! Someone who wasn't so bad that they could be fired without a long haul through target-setting, proof of incompetence and the fear of an unlawful dismissal case. Where is Lord Sugar when you need him?

Many of the organisations I have worked for are very conscious of racism, gender equality and lesbian, bisexual, gay and transgender (LBGT) issues. I still notice however that prejudice slips through the walls erected to keep it out and organisations fail to pick the best candidates leaving the door open to time-servers with no drive. On more than one occasion I have had to say, "Do you realise you have just eliminated all the candidates from ethnic minorities?" and then discovered that the "very good reasons" they had were spurious when carefully considered. This was generally accompanied by a lot of bluster to try and prove they were right all along and definitely never, ever racist. I remember showing a list of possible patrons to a member of a senior management team and being nonplussed at their claim that each of the ethnic minority candidates were not suitable patrons as they might get the organisation into trouble if they were found taking drugs! He didn't seem to realise which set of people he had chosen, neither could he articulate a reason other than something about them all being musicians, poets and actors.

Perhaps we might put that in the subconscious bracket where we may also park the uncomfortable truth that we all have a tendency to choose people we don't think will threaten our own position in the organisation. This acts as a broad dumbing-down of the organisation's talent pool and is recessive in that each iteration sees dumber people arriving. It is one of the key reasons for getting to grips with zombies in any senior position before they have the chance to replicate themselves by appointing even less energetic people. I must admit I sometimes react to people I think of as overachievers who I worry will either burn out or move on to better jobs very quickly. I also see them as people who are better than I am at quite a few things and therefore as competition.

Not all zombies arrive at the front door presenting as zombies. Many are driven to it by the organisation though things should never be allowed to get that far and we will look at this later in chapter 11: Are you a zombie?.

If you read any of the books on developing a great organisation, or growing your start-up, one of the key points raised is to surround yourself with excellent staff as they, perhaps even more than the mission or the product, are what make it a great organisation. Selecting them is the obvious first step though rewarding them properly is also key because you want them to stay and keep on delivering excellence across the organisation. Chapter 11: Are you a zombie? will also look at rewards in more detail.

Getting the right people on the bus

Without great people on board, organisations lose momentum, slow down their expansion and deliver a poorer and often increasingly reduced service. This is due not so much to losing their way; rather it is about a lack of inspiration and aspiration.

In the book *Good to Great* by Jim Collins, he uses the analogy of a bus which is stationary and notes that in the hundreds of companies he has studied, the ones that became great concentrated on first hiring the right people. Next they focussed on getting them into the right seats and getting the wrong people off the bus and then, and only then, they looked at where the bus is going next. Great people want to join exciting teams and join them on their journey, so we are faced with both the task of identifying and removing zombies, but crucially also the task of replacing them with first-rate people. Keeping the top people on board is much easier if your organisation is not stuffed full of indolent zombies asleep at their desks.

Jim also talks about the flywheel effect, which is that change is not about instant results, a sudden revelation or a magic solution, but about the slow and steady change which new people bring about incrementally as they engage with each aspect of their work. This is rather like getting an immensely heavy but stationary flywheel moving. It takes time and effort to get the first slow revolution going, but with persistent pressure over time the wheel revolves faster and faster until its momentum is unstoppable.

When you have removed the zombies, selected the right team and put them in the right jobs, the next step is to draw up the plans with them and build a great organisation by articulating a vision of the future, demonstrating the practical steps to get there and evaluating exactly how the beneficiaries' lives have been improved as a result. And of course it is important to see what could be done to make the service even better.

One of the key times in an organisation's life is when the founder who has driven the organisation forward retires or dies. They have often surrounded themselves with people who are competent at carrying out orders and getting things done but they lack the founder's vision. They struggle to think of new alternatives and cannot offer solutions when the organisation meets new trials or crises. Sometimes they cannot even think of the possibility of doing things differently and in our rapidly changing world, organisations led by such people are doomed. Many of these old-school founders started charities because of their war experience, which traumatised them and made them ruthless. They resemble survivors of post-traumatic stress disorder who are over-controlling with their children (though others are far too lax).

Often these organisations resemble zombie charities as the trustees and the chair are there because they knew the founder and because they could be trusted to keep the flame of the one true path alive. Unfortunately that makes it hard for them to hire the right people and to initiate changes that may be essential to keep the organisation afloat, effective and efficient.

If the organisation cannot bring in first-rate people, especially a new CEO, then it is in serious trouble, but fortunately it is straightforward to find good advice and there are any number of recruitment agencies who can help. There is a lot of really useful information on the Internet about searching for real talent. Any competent chair of the board will take advice and realise that acting professionally is essential, starting with finding the right CEO, then helping them through the process of making the whole organisation more effective.

Thinking outside the tick box

Have you read the biography of Howard Hughes or seen the film *The Aviator*? There is a tale told of how Hughes interviewed for his finance director. Instead of asking the usual questions he asked, "How does a battleship sight its guns?" so that the applicant would have to think through problems instead of giving an answer from experience. More recently Google developed a system of questions with obscure answers (or indeed no right answer at all) and found that this enabled them to choose between a set of highly qualified overachievers and find the right person for the job. Consider this from *Are You Smart Enough to*

Work at Google? by William Poundstone: "You are shrunk to the height of a penny and thrown into a blender. Your mass is reduced so your density is the same as usual. The blades start moving in sixty seconds. What do you do?" Apparently answering "Pray" won't get you the job! In a similar vein, "How many golf balls will fit in a 747?"

No zombies have been detected lurking at Google as far as I know, though reading about their current practice in *Wired* magazine, it appears they have unfortunately abandoned this sort of question and now use structured interviews with most questions having quantifiable answers.

I think most of us could improve our interview procedures by taking more time to engage with our interviewees' thought processes and stepping outside the rigid grid and revolving-door interview, where candidates tend to blur into each other after a while and plausible zombies can sidle through undetected.

We may also find some of those candidates who don't have the 'right' experience actually have experience which would enable them to come up to speed pretty quickly. This avoids re-advertising as well as dredging the bottom of the bucket for a new list of incompetents.

Maybe people who have done something other than climb a career ladder can cope with the challenge of the non-profit world today better than the 'right' candidate, but we may need to evolve new tools to find and test the suitability of such people.

Recruitment practice

Taking a logical look at recruitment practice shows that there is a series of steps following the decision that a new staff member is really needed. I think these also apply to the recruitment of volunteers; why should you have stringent criteria for staff and then not bother so much with volunteers, when it is important to have the right people in the right jobs capable of performing those tasks properly?

As well as taking the right steps you should have an equal opportunities policy; if you do not then write and agree one well before you start recruitment. If you do, read it and follow it as it will help you enormously to recruit the best team.

So the stages are:

- Preparation: What criteria should you use to hire people?
- Marketing the position: How do you advertise to reach the right people?
- Selecting from the applicants: Designing the application forms and shortlisting

- Interviewing: This is the core of the exercise, but depends on the stages above for its success
- Choosing the right person: Sticking to the criteria and checking references (using the phone helps to get accurate references)
- Other checks: Do you need a Disclosure and Barring Service (DBS) or Criminal Records Bureau (CRB) check for those working with children or vulnerable adults or supervising medical examinations?

Preparation

The key documents here are the job description (JD) and the person specification. The JD needs to outline each area of the job that the person might be engaged in, and should include a line to say they may be asked to undertake other tasks as requested by their line manager i.e. the person they report to. It is a fatal error to have anyone report to more than one person as anyone who has worked in a matrix management system knows. The JD also sets out whom the person reports to and who reports to them. It usually has an opening paragraph which outlines the job. The first-rate people you are after will read this carefully and gain a strong impression of both the work and their management, so make sure this is not just an off-the-shelf document from your HR department.

Make sure you are asking only for skills needed to do the job because you will find much better people, who will stay, by not over-defining the search criteria. Set out your actual requirements carefully so they are as clear as possible. Also ensure you do not close the door to those who may come from disadvantaged backgrounds, and so may not have the perfect career path but have all the right skills. Which formal qualifications are actually essential and what length of experience is really needed?

Note which of the criteria are really essential and which are merely desirable.

Similarly, the person specification needs to say to the best prospective applicants: "We want you!" Make sure that it clearly reflects the qualities you are looking for to carry out the work outlined in the JD.

Decide how all this will be tested. Some information will come from their CVs and most of the person-specification criteria will be tested in the interview by targeted questions (of course, everyone must be asked the same questions). Do give people a practical test as well as asking questions, if the work depends on their written work. For example, if recruiting a trust fundraiser, ask them to write something. Ask those who will be speaking in public to make a short presentation. Practical tests are one of the best ways to measure ability as they are less prone to interviewers making their mind up in the first few minutes then trying to prove themselves right. Professor Frank Bernieri of Toledo University and two of his students researched and articulated this tendency in 2000. That confident smile and firm handshake may not belong to the best candidate.

Marketing the position

The third sector is blessed with a number of recruitment agencies and though their services are not cheap, it is well worthwhile paying for the recruitment of an excellent team that will transform your organisation.

Do advertise all positions inside and outside the organisation simultaneously. You may know who you want to do the job but there may be someone much better out there. Do use ethnic minority media, informal networks or other means of widening your search.

Obviously any advertisement must be consistent with the job description, person specification and your equal opportunities policy as well as any legal requirements. Do name the person whom applicants should contact and make sure that candidates understand exactly what is required of them. Make sure HR has appropriate materials to send out.

If you are looking for exceptional people, and we should all be, then LinkedIn, Facebook, Twitter and other social media networks are good places to search. Social media is an ideal place to look for the best prospective candidates as they are advertising themselves (though not necessarily, of course, to find work) and those with a large following may well be doing something right in the field, if not leading it.

We do all Google candidates on our shortlist and sometimes our longlist, do we not? This is unstructured and can be dangerous as one can't believe everything that is revealed or see things that have been suppressed, like murder or fraud convictions, but it can also be very useful. The real difficulty is that it replaces those first five minutes of the interview, when we make up our minds, with us making up our minds online because someone appears like someone we want to meet, and then we may spend the interview trying to prove they are the best person. Can all the interviewers trust each other not to use Google first? And what happens if the interviewee is in one of our social networks? Naturally we should declare an interest if we know someone, but in an ever-increasingly interconnected world the chances of one of the interviewees knowing someone is steadily closing on 100%.

Choosing the right person

First, shortlist the candidates according to the essential criteria, then on the desirable ones. Ask more questions if you need to and write down your decisions and why you made them. This may become crucial later if you have to defend a decision. Do have your answers graded – think about what constitutes an acceptable answer, but more importantly what is the outstanding answer you are really looking for? This will also help if the interviewees ask about it later. Be prepared to give constructive feedback and to explain your decision.

Put the candidates at their ease before and after the interview and let them know when you will contact them and keep to that date.

Make sure your interview panel contains a broad selection of people for example look at ethnic minorities, gender, age etc. as this often gives a crucial advantage in finding the best candidate. Do give enough time between interviews to discuss the candidates, as you may find there are a number of helpful perspectives. Laslo Bock, Senior Vice-President of People Operations at Google, likes to have the people who will report to an interviewee being part of the interview panel. He also says that 80% of the people interviewed at Google who don't get the job would recommend their friends apply to Google.

In the interview, stick to the questions already decided unless supplementary questions are needed to elucidate an answer, and stick to the person who you agreed would ask particular questions rather than flitting from one panel member to another. It is surprisingly useful to score the answers out of a set number, for example ten, as remembering the answers that the first candidate gave at the end of the afternoon or the next day is nearly impossible. Scoring answers against each other builds an objective way of considering one candidate above another. Concentrate on the selection criteria in making your decision.

When you have decided on the most likely candidates, always check their references and call up referees to chat with them. They are far more likely to tell you the truth in a chat over the phone than when filling out a form. Always ask if they would employ that person again as this can be the most revealing question. Also be prepared for your top candidate to have applied for several other jobs and to turn your offer down so make sure you have an alternative, or two if other candidates have also passed your criteria.

It is sometimes necessary to re-advertise a position but in that case do think through just why the right candidates did not apply. It may well be that something in the preparation or process was not quite right and an unfortunate phrase may have sent out the wrong signal. It may be useful to ask someone to talk through the whole process with you.

Induction

You may hire the greatest talent on the planet but the first step in ensuring they can perform properly is the induction process. It is also the first step in ensuring that they don't evolve into zombies. Active care and positive management of new staff is essential in making people feel at home, making them part of the team and gaining their long-term commitment to the organisation and its goals.

The induction process is not just giving them a stack of policies and an organigram to read, then pointing out the fire escape or asking the first person available to show them around. It takes place over a period of weeks. Its length and content depend on the role that they will play in the organisation, what they need to know and who they need to meet to become an effective and committed member of staff.

In setting out an induction programme, consider what they should know on the first day, in the first week, second week and subsequent months. It is easy to overload people with information which means it is never remembered, but it is also easy to explain why they need to know things. This makes information much easier to recall, and helps you to eliminate stuff which is not relevant or to move items to later in the programme.

The induction process is a great way for people to meet others in the organisation for the first time and if key people are given roles in the process they are more inclined to spend time getting to know the new member of staff. People learn in different ways and also teach in different ways, so introducing them to a variety of staff members helps to make the induction process effective. Some people prefer to talk, discuss and ask questions and others find it easier to read material.

Things like the organisation's policies and other written material can be put into a welcome pack (or staff handbook) as you would for a new supporter, but it should also be discussed in case they never actually get around to reading it. It is all too easy to get on with the job and put such things aside for later, and later never comes.

An obvious but surprisingly often-neglected step is simply to tell the new person when to arrive and to have someone there to greet them and show them around. I also know from experience that it is easy to forget to tell other staff that someone new is starting and a little about them, which really helps to give them a favourable first impression.

We often forget that new arrivals may need some formal training quite early on, for example in using a database that is new to them. Organisations often regard training as a perk if people perform well, but the sense that one has been left alone to struggle on with tasks that require specialist explanation is demotivating and can be the start of disillusionment with the organisation.

For staff joining charities there is often an expectation that they are joining a lifestyle organisation, where everyone works together in harmony, caring for one another with everyone dedicated to the cause. It can be the biggest shock of someone's life to discover that the organisation they may have wanted to work in for years, and in which they have spent many hours volunteering, is actually riven with various alternative views, negativity and infighting, just like many other groups of humans jostling together. The campaigning organisations I have worked for are particularly prone to see internal campaigns waged as fiercely as those directed externally. A word of warning to new staff may just take the edge off this particular problem.

If these behaviours are rife in your organisation you have a problem that needs to be addressed urgently and action should be taken throughout the hierarchy. A proper way to resolve disputes and differences should be agreed with penalties for those who do not follow the rules. The whole thing should be introduced to staff, both in writing and also in groups or individually, depending on the organisation's size and structure.

Avoiding zombie hires – a short checklist

If you are looking at a CV, which is still the key document on which we rely in deciding who to interview, then there are some telltale signs to watch out for. What happens for example when you match their past employment against their referees? If they have recently worked for five years for the same non-profit but they don't give the director or their immediate boss as a reference, find out why. It could be that they have two or three other great references but it could also be that they hung on, limpet-like, refusing to be budged and performing way under par for the job. Of course five years in one position is generally a very good sign, especially outside the early career years when people tend to move around quite often before settling down. A CV where someone has moved on every eighteen months or two years for a long time tends to indicate that they have been moved on because they could not perform adequately, as it takes about that time to find out someone is rubbish and get them out of the job.

Do conduct practical tests at interview if at all possible, and set questions that have measurable results so that you can clearly compare candidates. Try having people from other departments at the interview because they may be more objective and consider personality as much as performance, as they do not have your immediate objectives playing on their mind. Pay real attention to equal opportunities as this widens the scope of your search and can bring in exceptional candidates who may not be on your radar or that of your recruitment company or where you usually advertise.

Always check references carefully. This is not the formality that people think it is and can be revealing but only if you take it seriously and chat to referees to find out exactly what the candidate was like when they worked for the referee. "Would you hire them again?" is the key question and any hesitation here should worry you.

Selecting the right people for the job is obviously the starting point, but it is how they are introduced into the organisation and how they are then treated which will determine to a large extent whether the right people become part of the team or part of the problem in their early years.

Think about the position and how it might change over the next few years. The key question to ask yourself is, "Is this person the right one for the future?" and try not to be swayed by the urgent need to replace, say, that staff member that left suddenly and whose post you really need to fill immediately. We live in changing times and people often need to be more adaptable than in the past. Is this position one that needs a steady hand and will not alter much over the years, or is it one that is going to evolve and needs someone to evolve with it? If you put a dynamic person in a steady style of job they may leave, but worse they may just stay, disillusioned, brooding and angry.

4 Zombie fundraising techniques

An old friend used to run an annual ball for a small charity. It got off to a flying start because she knew the right people and enlisted some of her mother's friends to the organising committee. They quickly set up a series of subcommittees to sell tables, which they did within a few weeks as they were all calling in favours from when they had bought tables at other charity events. The event was held in an upmarket hotel, the food and atmosphere were great and everyone danced until midnight. Most of the board of trustees attended, brought their spouses and loved the fact that the charity could host such a grand event so successfully.

The next year the event was given a budget that required 10% more profit though no extra expenditure was allocated. The organising committee duly attracted some prestigious names and the event was another roaring success. The organisers had the benefit of the previous year's experience and the original attendees knew it was going to be fun so they came again bringing their friends with them. The event was growing rapidly.

In the third year the expected profit was again 10% higher with no extra money to spend and my friend introduced a silver auction at the end of the dinner, with some jewellery from a well-known silversmith. The ball went very well and actually exceeded its income target. By now it was close to being the organisation's main source of income although it had become very time-consuming, with the organisation for the next ball beginning pretty much as soon as the last ball ended. Seats at the top table, which hadn't really been very significant, now became prized possessions and the chair of the board, a rather pompous individual, insisted on sitting next to the chair of the organising committee, and bringing several business colleagues and their partners to the table without paying. The reasoning was that the organisation could tap them for sponsorship later. Later of course never came and certainly didn't involve the chair lifting a finger to help.

Reaching tipping point

The fourth and fifth years were pivotal as my anxious friend, aware that expectations were beginning to outgrow reality, tried to keep the targets realistic. But each year the expected profit grew. The fact that the fourth year's income had not grown, and had indeed been slightly under the previous year's total, was seen as a black mark on her record by some, and a mere aberration to be righted the following year by others. What was really happening, as my friend pointed out, was that the original high-powered committee members had moved on – some because they were annoyed by the chair, though they were far too polite to mention it. What's more the whole ball scene was shifting to less formal events and the charity itself was not one that commanded great respect among those who might attend a ball of such a scale and cost to attend. The tickets had gone from £75 each to £280 for two, with no single tickets available.

Not for the first time, my friend put forward a more comprehensive fundraising strategy with a variety of events and a scaling-back of the ball, which had somehow acquired the title of 'The Grand Ball'. Unfortunately the CEO who liked the plan could not get the honorary treasurer to agree (pressure from the chair was at play). By now this meant compensating for the organisation's past under-investment in fundraising and consequently laying off some programme staff. My friend left and a new experienced staff member was brought in especially to run the ball which was given additional expenditure for the first time, but with a very large income target. Much of the additional income went on advertising which was professionally done by a PR company who said they could buy space very cheaply and get leaflets into hotels and other venues.

Unfortunately the event had reached a tipping point and numbers were heavily down, with some people feeling the event had been cheapened by the new marketing programme. The profit was all but wiped out by the expenditure and the charity had to lay off more staff anyway. This was done equally across the board with each department losing the same number of staff, much to the incredulity of the fundraising department, who explained that if their staff were cut the income would go down even further the following year. The explanation fell on deaf ears and the organisation suffered another drop in income. The Grand Ball was, however, still expected to save the day and to return to its former glory the following year or perhaps the one after that. For all I know it is still lurching on, crippling the organisation but kept alive by optimism and arrogance.

These days such balls are less likely to be the mainstays of fundraising events as they have been overtaken by a plethora of other activities. Rock concerts too followed a similar trajectory and grew to outlandish proportions until they in turn collapsed leaving fundraisers rather more sanguine about the growth potential of concerts. Their colleagues in other departments often don't share their reluctance as such concerts have wide appeal across the non-profit world and there is a desire to keep them going for the publicity, donor cultivation and the general fun of running high-profile events and rubbing shoulders with celebrities.

My friend has now joined a consultancy, which gives her the flexibility to juggle childcare and holidays, yet she is still encountering similar problems with some of her client organisations. She reckons that many of the great causes she is asked to help do not really have a fundraising problem, rather a management or governance problem. This usually becomes clear very early on when she starts to discuss how the organisation raises its funds. Fortunately she is well equipped in matters of management and governance and, once the organisation has established an agreed fundraising strategy and action plan, communications between fundraisers and management usually get back to normal pretty quickly. This may sound easy but is no mean feat as it involves a great deal of emotional intelligence and the ability not to trade away key desirables to get an agreement.

Be strategic – make the world a better place!

My twenty years' work as a consultant has taught me that it is so much easier for someone outside the organisation to raise difficult issues because they have no axe to grind and have the respect of all parties in the process. The key here is not just to look at the one technique that may be going wrong. The question the consultant is brought in to answer may be: "How can we make more money from X?" but they should be asked to look at it in the context of all the fundraising techniques employed and the organisation's programme strategy for the next few years. The question the consultant should be asked then becomes: "How can we raise more money to fund the programme work?" and the answer is an organisation-wide fundraising strategy fully costed and scheduled. The key to making it all work lies in an action plan attached to the new fundraising strategy that sets out who does what and when, so that everyone knows the role they have to play as well as the actual activities broken down into SMART objectives (specific, measurable, agreed, realistic and timed). At that point there is a manageable process in place which can be measured and evaluated, not just according to the income raised by one fundraising technique but also by the timeliness and effectiveness of all the agreed actions taken during the whole lifespan of the fundraising strategy.

From time spent in senior management discussions I recognise that other techniques in an organisation are just as likely as fundraising ones to turn into zombies. It is just that zombie fundraising techniques are most noticeable because when they lose money it has far greater repercussions than when, say, a finance department uses hopelessly out-of-date software year after year because the head of finance doesn't want to retrain or allow their staff to do so. The effect of that may be disastrous but invisible. Similarly when money is steadily pumped into a village in a developing country to, say, build wells and a school, and this simply replaces money that the local administration would have spent. Again who would know unless there is a great field officer who understands the local power structures?

This is not a counsel of despair but a nudge on the road to very thorough monitoring and evaluation. We know the positive outcomes that are possible from what happens when major clothing companies resolve to deal with appalling factory conditions overseas. It is difficult to implement but absolutely key to ensure sustainable change. At first the factory owners are able to fool companies year after year but gradually they are forced to impose better monitoring systems.

In the end those new monitoring and evaluation skills make for better livelihoods, improved corporate responsibility and a better impact in the world. Of course, this is often led by campaigning groups driving these improvements.

When decisions fly in the face of the facts

Events, in particular, have a special inclination to flip over into sudden-death syndrome, becoming unprofitable from one year to the next. This happens when events look healthy having grown rapidly from year to year. Little wonder then that senior management greets news of threats to an event with some incredulity. Everyone enjoys them, your boss takes her husband, communications extols them in the media and membership fondly believes they make a difference. But events typically reach a size when the expectations for growth become unsustainable and people just do not turn up. The result is a failure to meet budget *and* an actual and often significant financial loss.

Unfortunately, this is not an isolated occurrence and though events are probably the most high-profile casualty in fundraising departments they are not the only fundraising practice that has turned into a zombie. There are often others, dead on their feet, lurching on from year to year, their income falling, their costs rising and their return on investment (ROI) heading south. Yet for some inexplicable reason they will neither die nor wander off and cease to trouble the professional fundraiser!

Whilst any technique returns even a semblance of a profit it is often hard to get CEOs and boards to agree its demise. The technique has a budget line all to itself and you may be expected to add, say, 10% to its profit each year and to provide a detailed description of how this will be done. Sounds familiar? Just say, "No" quite a few times at all stages of the process and explain exactly why: because the people who keep zombie techniques going really do not understand fundraising or indeed how business works. Often the money tied up in a zombie technique could be used to start a new fundraising venture but convincing treasurers that innovative techniques are likely to become profitable in a few years when the zombie is still making a profit now (however small) is a hard sell.

Sometimes the power of a well-expressed rationale for changing fundraising techniques or activities can change minds, but it often requires persistence and faith that persuasion works in the face of great odds. The inertia and sheer ignorance of many civil society organisations mean that the dice are stacked against you. Getting your innovative thoughts and suggestions down in writing so that you have a paper trail can be a lifesaver, or at least a job saver, as we all know who is likely to be blamed when a zombie technique brings down staffing levels or projects.

Sometimes the maths behind zombie techniques is suspect and the real ROI is hidden in off-budget costs such as meetings time, support from other parts of the organisation and marketing agencies adding a large percentage to things like printing.

All of which shows how zombie techniques acquire an illusion of being alive. They may require a huge amount of maintenance on your part, taking your time and energy from techniques where performance could be improved.

Zombies in the making

Many people suspect direct mail is not quite in the land of the living but staggers about on the border about to fall over at any moment. This type of proto-zombie requires very careful observation as huge parts of it may become unprofitable quickly and need to be axed. This in turn may increase unit costs and so steadily increase the pressure on the remaining elements even though they may be valid income-generators for some time to come. For example, if you are mailing one million direct mail packs a year and notice that three-quarters of your mailing lists are unproductive, you may cut the mailing back to 250,000 packs. But then the same costs of copywriting etc. remain and so the unit cost rises, perhaps making another 100,000 packs unproductive. This goes on until you, hopefully, reach a much smaller but profitable core of excellent mailing lists.

Sometimes the astrologers take over and your assessment of proto-zombies and their tendency to flatline depends on the arcane rituals of lifetime value, legacy potential and volunteering value. These cannot be ignored but are very hard to quantify and require a high level of mathematical understanding to predict with any accuracy. When this happens listening to the top experts on these calculations rather than, say, your finance department's guess, becomes all-important.

Applications for grants to trusts, foundations and government are often one of the key pillars of an organisation's fundraising and with an ROI in the area of 1:10 it is hard for them to become an unkillable zombie technique. However they do tend to enter the doldrums with the same proposals being sent out year after year to an ever-widening circle of trusts that are never going to respond. Then when a recession hits and trusts' ability to give is severely affected by a downturn in interest rates (their own investments being not as productive as they were) the first charities to lose their grants are those that send out boring, monotonous zombie-like applications. I have known this to be so bad that an organisation with three staff in its trust department (essentially a head of department that was coasting and two assistants he didn't need) became a loss-making unit, which took eighteen months to turn around.

Major donor fundraising is another area where the ROI is so high, again about 1:10, that it is hard to see how it could ever fail; but it has its own particular way of turning into a zombie practice and that is inherent in one of its few rules. With wealthy people we are advised to first cultivate them, then when they are ready (which they may indicate by mentioning a desire to give) to ask for a significant sum. The problem being that we have a built-in reluctance to ask anyone for a significant sum, just as they have an inbuilt reluctance to offer such sums; unless they were brought up in the US culture where legend has it that respect in a community comes not from the mere possession, or acquisition, of wealth but its use to help that community. In the UK this means that cultivation goes swimmingly and we are all great friends but that 'ask' disappears into a very hazy future whilst the staff and cultivation event costs rise inexorably to strangle the ROI.

Personally I blame zombie management that just slaps a percentage increase on each income stream and refuses to listen to reason in the budget-setting process. This unsustainable incremental growth in expectation is a silent killer that will eventually terminate any technique. As we have seen, events tend to be the canary in this particular mine, being prone to sudden collapse.

Heroic management

On the other hand, heroic management will ascertain which techniques are going to become key income streams over the next few years and invest appropriately in nurturing their growth. For them this is a key part of the budgeting process and allows for a more confident prediction about revenue in the medium term. It also allows for a more informed discussion about the allocation of future income in the long term. Programme or campaigns staff are less inclined to argue for investment in fundraising to be stifled once they realise the drastic effect such decisions will have on the organisation's future expenditure. A management that is prepared to steer investment away from failing techniques, axe posts and techniques if they are not productive, is like the wise gardener pruning the roses and composting the failures. But like the gardener, management must understand the process of growth and death in order to be successful, especially when it comes to the maths of fundraising and the psychology of giving. Unfortunately above the level of a departmental head of fundraising that knowledge is often lacking which is one reason why zombie techniques may emerge and refuse to die.

Nina Saffuri, Director of Fundraising at War Child UK, was reported in *Fundraising Magazine,* May 2015, as saying, "Concerts are expensive and we have to consider ROI so we are not looking to create more of that type of event as part of our growth strategy at all." This is brave coming from a charity that the article noted "was becoming synonymous with music and music events", but strikes just the right note when looking at growth and the development of apparently valuable relationships as a result of events.

Looking at the future, Nina pointed to the success of their partnership with Aviate Global. In the previous year the relationship had raised £350,000 in funds that were not for a specific project and which highlight just what can be achieved if ambition and imagination predominate. One of the key elements that will keep this relationship from becoming a zombie is the company's demand for impact reporting, as that keeps all parties on their toes, and ensures that the funds are spent well.

The donor knows if anything is amiss, which is bound to be the case from time to time in the field, but will be educated in the realities of the charity's work.

The speed of the Net

For several years, the bright new area for fundraising investment has been in social media and mobile-based techniques, though the smash-and-grab techniques of direct marketing when applied to Internet fundraising have proved remarkably unsuitable to social media. Nonetheless we have seen an unaccustomed patience behind such investment which is now beginning to pay off through the development of tools such as JustGiving to link donors to their friends when they run races or go on walks for charity, for example, and affinity marketing where donors buy goods online and a percentage goes to their chosen charity. Crowdfunding and SMS campaigns have proved very effective with some going viral, none of which would have happened without considerable investment over time. Even so the sector has largely failed to learn the lessons of Avaaz (www.avaaz.org) and similar extraordinary start-ups, whose sites look nothing like conventional charities, but which have raised millions of pounds in remarkably few years.

The speed of change of the Internet means that we may soon see the first of its zombie techniques emerge as more investment is ploughed into an unproductive idea or piece of technology. The Internet is littered with zombie platforms like MySpace, a host of other defunct social networks and other debris. So far organisations have been able to simply move on to new or improved techniques when for example early software for affinity marketing proved ineffective (because people had to go to a separate website before ordering goods). Now, once an app has been downloaded, an appropriate purchase gives the charity a percentage of the price paid.

The power to transform

Even more important is the way that an organisation thinks about and handles fundraising. In many organisations everyone is expected or at least encouraged to take part in campaigning, or in helping out with the programme work, and if the same expectation was applied to fundraising we would see a much greater understanding leading to far fewer mistakes. This is not to encourage everyone to take part in a flag day, walk or coffee morning, excellent though that might be, but for everyone to consider helping fundraising in broad terms as part of their work. This may be researchers or campaigners helping to prepare applications to grant-makers, trustees speaking to wealthy people they know and public speakers for the organisation asking influential people they meet to come to events. It is also about being prepared to make introductions and work on those six degrees of separation to reach the 1% who own more than half the world's wealth.

Some time ago I was told that the Dalai Lama was advocating a large scheme and when he was asked where the money would come from he carefully replied, "From where it is now." 'Where it is now' is in the hands of a very rich band of people who have prospered far more than the middle classes for some considerable time. This gives major donor fundraisers an unprecedented opportunity to raise very large sums and to transform their organisations; however, as we have seen, the whole process is often mired in a culture so lacking in ambition that the number of zombies in the field is spreading fast; we may soon need to clone Buffy to survive.

Part of this particular problem is that those who work in the non-profit sector are suspicious if not antagonistic towards the seriously rich, so building bridges and personally engaging with them is far from their minds. This is alarming as we are about to see a vast transference of wealth from at least a hundred billionaires who have accepted Bill Gates's challenge to sign the 'giving pledge' to donate half their wealth in their lifetime, or when they die. More so as we know that others are about to follow suit rather than bequeathing all their wealth to their children. This is one area where we absolutely cannot afford to let our techniques atrophy.

Heroic management

Heroic management is best led from the top with the chair and honorary treasurer taking the lead in ensuring that the whole fundraising programme is productive, adequately funded and supported by a vision to grow new fundraising techniques as old ones fall from productivity. At board level this can make a huge difference particularly when trustees are both well connected and passionate about the cause. The board's lead feeds down to the director and so to senior management level and this can avoid a silo mentality whereby each manager is fighting for their own corner particularly during the budget process. When each manager has an understanding and appreciation of fundraising, in the same way they often do for the organisation's programme work, there is the basis for a transformation of the organisation's income. This in turn can lead to a revitalisation of the organisation itself and its ability to achieve its mission.

I have also seen the amazing effect of fundraising directors who were impressive figures and had the respect of the organisation behind them. These individuals really changed the organisations where they worked internally in terms of professionalism and externally in terms of the huge amounts of money raised. These are my heroes and behind every great organisation you will not have to look far to spot a great fundraiser who freed the fundraising programme from a lack of imagination and a fear of fundraising. This fear is prevalent in so many organisations that it often passes undetected as normal scrutiny; but it manifests itself in keeping alive zombie techniques to prevent other ways of raising funds from being used. This often emerges as a personal dislike of a technique expressed in terms of, "My mother hates street fundraising," or "The chair will be dead-set against this, let's postpone it till next year".

Zombie fundraising techniques are like the worm that eats the apple, often unseen until they have caused untold damage not least by lowering the morale of fundraisers and consequently their drive and impact.

Spotting a zombie technique

If you think you have a zombie fundraising technique on your hands test it against the list of signs below. If you find just one item applies you have a problem; if you have two your boss has a problem and if you have three your organisation is in trouble. It's time to sharpen that axe in the basement. The technique is a zombie if:

- It loses money but staggers on from budget to budget.
- It eats the money that you would like to see invested in new techniques that never emerge.
- It swaggers around being praised by everyone, but has bandages wrapped around its feet and the expected

number of participants or predicted income becomes completely unrealistic.
- It's referred to as 'old fashioned'; you call it 'dead on its feet'.
- If you suggest shutting it down, people quote a supposedly important person who wouldn't like that.
- If it appears again next year, you wouldn't like that.
- If it appears the year after that as well, you might be in another job.

Having realised that we may need to make radical changes, it is well worth checking to see if we need to garner support at a senior level before wielding the axe. Fortunately many fundraising techniques have more opponents than friends and, however mistaken their reasons for that opposition, it is useful that they are in effect backers for change. High-profile events garner adherents who have strong, if illogical, reasons to keep them running and they may emerge as fierce defenders in the face of an existential threat. In the latter case having a supporter at senior management or even trustee level can make a huge difference.

Looking on the positive

Do you have the investment required to move into the next big thing and to test out some of the possibilities that are rising in the fundraising firmament? If you do, then this may be where you should concentrate your effort, especially if ending a technique will prove to be a huge struggle. If you have the nerve it may be wisest to let the technique reveal its lack of profitability beyond the slightest doubt before making your move. The chances are the only criticism you will hear is, "You should have seen that coming!" Starting new ideas is far more fun and likely to have positive backing if funds are in the budget and may exceed the potential losses if you let another budget line run into the red. These days new ideas tend to be social media or major donor related and either can be hugely profitable.

However, few of us in this sector have the luxury of ample money to invest. What's more there is a mindset that thinks of fundraising as a necessary evil instead of the engine that drives the development of the organisation and allows other parts to grow and deliver their services. Fortunately we fundraisers are tough-skinned and able to weather colleagues taking a pop at fundraising in a way that they never would with other departments.

The crack in the dam...

Zombie fundraising techniques occur when a method of fundraising ceases to be profitable, or when it makes very little profit but prevents funds being invested in better ideas. Often this is because it offers non-financial rewards to senior members of the organisation or financial rewards to other parts of the organisation. This is often true of events that linger on way past their sell-by date. Sometimes techniques become zombies due to bad budgeting, for example, when each budget line is expected to increase by X per cent every year regardless of how realistic this may be.

Ending zombie techniques may take quite a lot of courage especially if they have high-level backing, but a clear knowledge of the facts and figures will undoubtedly bring you support at whatever level is necessary.

A close look at other parts of the organisation could also reveal a nest of zombie techniques so scrutiny should be directed not just at high-profile events but also at finance, communications and programme work too.

Zombie fundraising techniques can be rather like the crack in the dam: if left then the whole organisation may be in trouble. If it is a simple case of one technique keeling over then that is probably not too hard to deal with, as its financial impact may cost the organisation a few jobs. The question is could this be indicative of a general malaise and will this herald more income streams drying up? The question to ask is, "Why has it happened?" When you know the answer to that it might just lead you to consider other techniques; indeed you might also consider auditing just about everything else, perhaps bringing in someone external who does not have a vested interest in preserving certain techniques. The cost of this may be high but the cost of doing nothing can be catastrophic, as the fight to preserve a technique may result in good people leaving and good money being thrown after bad until the organisation has a much more serious problem.

Sometimes, the problem is one where it is easy to justify an organisation's income staying about the same for quite some time because, say, national GDP is not growing and the economy is not doing very well. Because few non-fundraisers have a really good feel for fundraising, one or more zombie techniques may go unnoticed until they present a real threat to the organisation's income.

Lastly, an obvious point, but fundraising techniques are there to raise funds. If they don't do that but, say, give the organisation profile then they should not be in the fundraising department but in the communications department or wherever else is reaping the benefit.

5 Zombie communications

More than ever before, communications departments play a crucial role in charities. The speed with which social media and other online communications are evolving and the need to keep members, supporters and donors in touch and engaged means that communications teams have to be on top of their game. Teams cannot, however, de-prioritise television and selected print media; rather these channels too have to be integrated alongside the online activity to meet their demand for news, information and entertainment. The other factor making professional communications vital for charities is the media's exposure of failure, bad practice in governance and unacceptable fundraising practices, all of which may need to be competently and sensitively rebutted when the media come knocking at your own door.

It may be salutary to look back at the time when the Internet first impacted non-profits and the golden era of zombie communications departments that refused to engage. Unfortunately in many organisations little has changed. I hear people saying they are waiting for the Internet fad to pass, or nowadays the social media fad. One problem is that with departments like finance and fundraising it is easy to set targets but for others like communications it can be very difficult. So we don't bother and any mention in the press is a cause for excitement as perhaps it should be when the press often reports so little on our sector.

Some years back, when I was running an organic farming association, I wondered for ages why our press releases never got anywhere and so I spent some more time perfecting them. And then I spent some more time again. Yes, I know they are not the greatest form of communication but there was nary a mention anywhere in the media until one day when I personally checked the press list itself and found it was hopelessly out of date. The public affairs department had never updated it. Many of our stories were going to staff who had left years back and key publications were not even on the list. That set me thinking and I began to realise that there were relatively few journalists that I really wanted to reach, so I invited them out to lunch just to find out what they were looking for and discovered that worked far better than the press releases ever had. It wasn't cheap and it often involved way too much alcohol, but it worked and the conversations were often amazing. These days the food is much better and the alcohol unnecessary.

Hazel worked in the PR department of a rival charity to mine during the 90s and was deeply frustrated because its promotional work just didn't function effectively. She could see our publicity, campaigning and brand soaring but couldn't quite figure out why we were having so much more impact than her own unit. It did not take too much working out: when her boss went to the effort of taking journalists to lunch he went without his briefing and came back in the afternoon inebriated, often sleeping in a corner of his office. His staff welcomed his absence as he was a rather forbidding character having been a seasoned reporter on a national daily. He would wander into their offices reeking of tobacco smoke, to regale them with long, though admittedly amusing, anecdotes about his past.

The final nail in her department's coffin came when both organisations were affected by a scandal in our industry and my organisation bounded back, having an agreed crisis policy that we could put into effect immediately. In addition our staff were prepared to work at night when required and found it exciting to engage with journalists, whether they were from the press or television or even the early Internet outlets. The response from Hazel's organisation was stalled until the director returned from holiday, as no one else was authorised to act, and the director wouldn't go within a mile of a television studio. All of which had the unfortunate effect of making them appear part of the problem as they were saying "No comment" when they should have been responding and putting their arguments across. During Tony Blair's premiership, Alastair Campbell's very effective Labour Party rebuttal unit really brought home the importance of getting a message out quickly and unequivocally to protect the reputation of an organisation.

The other factor that held back Hazel's department and which prevented them from being effective was the fact that the research department would not agree to the wording of anything the PR department wanted to say. They were academics and very good at their job but hopeless at communicating to the public. And what was worse, they had captured the ear of the director whose background in research meant that he was frightened of misrepresenting the organisation's findings, hence his avoidance of the TV studios.

Slowly the PR department lost the will to even struggle to seize the day or for that matter the week or month. The organisation's campaigns became great academic studies in the subject matter and had a life in academic literature; but as far as changing hearts and minds, let alone the facts on the ground or reaching into the media, they were frankly useless.

Sitting across the corridor from the PR department was one very frustrated head of fundraising. She really needed the public to know, understand and appreciate the organisation before she approached them for a donation. As her donor recruitment programme grew, fundraising effectively became the PR vehicle for the organisation due to the sheer weight of the direct mail, loose-leaf inserts, door-to-door and face-to-face activities placing the work of the organisation in front of the public.

Enter IT...

As in many other organisations, the development of email, websites and blogs meant that the IT specialists had steadily more control over the content of communications materials as well as the hardware and software involved. In effect they became the organisation's Internet police and could baffle anyone out of anything to do with the Internet by the use of jargon. In general, this situation only lasted a few years as senior management fought to retake control from whichever department had IT in its team, which was often the finance department.

Hazel's team fought for a separation between the IT specialists (so that they would be a service department in finance) and a new communications department (that would give the old public affairs staffers control over content and the emerging Internet platforms). However, when the senior management team looked at the public affairs department in the light of the new environment they felt it was incapable of adapting and so the status quo prevailed to the despair of the communicators and the fundraisers. The following year the director moved the growing IT team into his own secretariat and shortly after brought Hazel in to write content to support various Internet opportunities. Gradually the PR department shrank. Although print media was still valuable it seemed almost impossible to have enough exposure to make it worthwhile employing more than one person. As that point approached, the head of PR left and Hazel was appointed as the head of communications taking over the PR and the IT teams. One of her first acts was to split duties between the new comms department and finance. The zombie department had finally been laid to rest.

These days the discussions are more about issues such as the advisability of having one organisational Twitter account instead of having everyone tweeting from their own department. And should the director actually write his own blog? Zombie communications departments are more likely to be found in those organisations that are not engaging at all in this kind of debate or that are really not aware of what people are saying online about their organisation or failing to integrate online and traditional communications activities. It is usually a mistake to think in terms of online or offline and thankfully we are back to thinking of communications as an integrated whole.

Hazel's view is that people are understandably reluctant to live in a state of permanent revolution and at some point they simply refuse or fail to adapt to changes and have to be let go. This is crucially important right now as the means of communication are in just such a state and failure to engage constantly with each new technique means a loss of market share in favour of those organisations that make them work. Hazel is clear that this is not to say each technique will be worth pursuing or last indefinitely and, of course, some will be dropped once people stop using them. Fortunately, she is energised by the excitement of engaging with each new concept as it emerges and especially when it drives supporter engagement across generations and social classes.

What's the damage?

Sometimes zombie communications are not so bad that a whole department ceases to engage in the new means of communicating and lies down and dies. Sometimes it is more that they engage half-heartedly and merely put what would have been in the unreadable press release into a Twitter feed, blog, Google+ or Facebook post that no one reads because it is basically very, very boring. It is one thing to engage by signing up and using a new technique, it is quite another to engage effectively and grow the organisation's base of supporters.

A rubbish comms department can destroy a healthy organisation, but because this can happen imperceptibly over a number of years, no one notices, and as the organisation fails to engage with new supporters or to appear in the media it slowly sinks from view, surrounded by boiled frogs. Even more importantly the organisation disappears from the hearts of all but its most valiant supporters. Sometimes this can be countered by the fundraising department with perhaps a larger budget, especially in regard to recruitment campaigns which tend to be very visible. Occasionally, comms and fundraising departments are merged, which only works if the head of the new department has a strong fundraising background as well as great comms skills because both are professions with different professional standards and responsibilities.

The morale of an organisation can be raised immensely by TV appearances or features in the press; TV particularly still has a huge reach and gravitas – which is sometimes lacking in a tweet, however many times it is retweeted. The feeling that the organisation is relevant and effective can transform staff from indolent proto-zombies into lively enthusiasts that can perform miracles. When effective communications-coverage across platforms coincides with a fundraising or social change campaign the response to both can be amazing.

When campaigns engage with a large body of supporters online and on TV then the results can be staggering with financial and campaign expectations being greatly exceeded. This can be easily seen when charities engage with A-list celebrity patrons persuading them to reach out to their Twitter or Facebook followers, who then send the message out to all their followers and pretty soon everyone in the universe has had a bucket of cold water dumped over their head.

Getting good content

One expects well-written copy and evocatively framed, compelling arguments to come out of a communications department as well as photos, videos and any other material that will raise the profile of the organisation, draw support for its work and help its development. However, the department can only be as good as the material it is supplied with from the field, or the researchers or specialists who work with the beneficiaries. This is the information pipeline and if it is of poor quality, does not operate in a timely way and it is a struggle for comms to get hold of the people responsible for that information then the whole organisation will suffer. Sometimes one department can have a stranglehold on the information flow and demand that the information they provide is delivered in the exact words in which it left their department. This is a nightmare for communicators and a dangerous tendency to which research and professional staff can be prone. The answer is that the level of management which covers both departments needs to establish the ground rules and ensure they are respected. As ever management needs to be firm but fair, and more importantly to favour the development of the whole organisation over the interests of any one department.

There is probably no quicker way to create a poorly performing comms department than to starve it of information per se, or of timely information. We only see the charities that are great communicators in the media, which can lead to unrealistic expectations for other comms departments that are asked to produce positive headlines about their charity that works in a disturbing area, such as conflict, where more consideration is required to get the message *exactly* right for the subject matter. For example, Greenpeace has boats of all sizes and could easily produce photos of their larger boats towering over those dumping waste at sea. Instead, they always feature boats that are much smaller than those of the other side so their people appear as brave heroes confronting a much larger enemy. For a time this was particularly effective as they sent out video reports which were lapped up by a grateful media, especially television, but was almost impossible for other organisations to emulate, despite everyone leaning on the comms teams to produce material that was as effective.

Sometimes organisations feature in the media, especially the 'red tops', for completely the wrong reasons, like a financial scandal. This can have several results, including better scrutiny of finance departments, though it can also generate a paranoid fear of bad publicity; this can paralyse organisations and ensure nothing leaves the comms department before being signed off by half the staff. There is little that people love more than changing other people's copy and trivial copy fights are one of the signs of a management team that is afraid to manage.

Communication is everyone's job and its importance needs to be explained and emphasised by management, so that the department does not sit in a silo unable to access the raw material of its craft.

Preventing the emergence of silos applies to each of the senior management teams, be that for communications, fundraising, campaigns, programmes in the field and even finance. The professionals in each department must not despise and denigrate each other or look at one part of the organisation as a necessary evil. Nor should departments think that they alone are the heroes and that others are merely bit players providing them with backup.

Let's be clear that this need for mutual respect between departments to make a healthy organisation also places demands on volunteers and trustees who may start with a very limited interest in one specific part of the organisation. It is vital they should gain a balanced view of the functions of all parts of the organisation and the importance of each element to the whole. This is best done right away with their induction into the organisation.

The damage to comms departments that leaves them as zombies may not be immediately obvious. It starts with a lack of publicity and often poor internal communication too. This makes the achievement of the organisation's overall goals much harder, though this may erroneously be put down to a recession or other changes in the organisation's environment. None of this may, however, become apparent until an effective comms character takes over the department and management plays its role properly in mediating between departments. Once this happens then the resultant rise in public awareness and support for the organisation as well as the rise in morale of the staff and volunteers can be seen and felt by everyone.

What's the solution?

Say we were going to build a communications department from scratch, where would we start? This may be a better approach than thinking about what we have and how it can be improved. Often a new dynamic head of department will have a very clear idea of the department they wish to see, and will steadily move to achieve that by setting the strategy so the whole department knows where it is going, then setting out the tasks (sometimes called objectives) and the milestones to achieving those tasks.

This is followed by working on the roles and job descriptions of the staff that need to be in place to get there, and finally allocating staff to the new posts or tweaking their existing roles to meet the new needs.

At this stage new people can be brought in and existing staff may be encouraged to move on. Where this is the object of the whole reorganisation it may amount to constructive dismissal and it may be much more efficient to look at staff whose profile no longer fits the new work and think in terms of their training and mentoring. Where the staff concerned have no interest in the available roles then dismissal may be the right way to go as they are effectively redundant.

As ever, planning which includes all levels of the organisation is crucial if you are to create a communications strategy and action plan that everyone will buy into and in which they will play an effective part. This starts with the CEO who should be open to communication across the organisation and not just with senior managers. The CEO and senior managers should also model the use of such communication and the use of social media so that staff can take their cues from this behaviour. This may require coaching for senior management in the same way that they may have training to be spokespeople (especially in talking to the media) almost as soon as they start. All this training is a key part of building a dynamic comms department. We are used to concentrating on the message but sometimes forget that the delivery of that message is just as important to ensure it is put across effectively, received correctly and acted upon.

Where a zombie department has been happily doing very little, very badly, for years, the personal resentment and anguish at a new approach may spill over into attempts to undermine the new director or whoever is leading the changes. These individuals will need the backing of those above them and often the board as well. I have been approached by board members who have told me not to get rid of a clearly incompetent staff member, in breach of good governance behaviour from members of a board that had earlier expressed agreement with the decision. I then received no support to fire the individual from the director or the deputy director who instead warned me not to antagonise the board!

Building trust across the department is crucial to its revival. People who have been stagnating will need the confidence to begin communicating again professionally and putting their heads over the parapet in a public way. If management trusts its people by giving them front-line roles where appropriate, rather than keeping such roles to themselves, they will begin to build an engaged team. This team may in turn develop a huge following for the organisation across the media and this presence may be far larger than anything the senior managers could have created on their own.

How can we tell if it's working? The answer to that is evaluation and though I have said it is not so easy with communications, it is crucial to stop and check that what one is doing is getting through and is building the kind of support that the communications strategy is seeking to cultivate. On one hand the measurement of column inches and what it would have cost to buy that space in the press, radio and TV and on the other the number of followers on Twitter or 'likes' on Facebook provide a simple measurement, which can be made periodically to see if the organisation is growing. Bear in mind that the quality of such measurements is equally important. Where has your communication been received? Who is following you? Are you reaching the target audience? Do you have agreed demographics and metrics for the target audience? Try building a performance hub with people outside the department to measure it and then to communicate the results internally. Part of great communication is taking the whole organisation with you and allowing internal communications to flourish too.

Talking about the target audience, is it segmented so that you can use the arguments that resonate with each segment? Do you also integrate campaigns across social and traditional media, perhaps with events and other activities that reach out to the segment you are interested in at that time?

Sometimes the glamour of new media can cause a comms department to effectively abandon the press, radio and television, which is another route to zombification. In certain cases an organisation may be built and grow rapidly online like Avaaz (www.avaaz.com) but to maximise effectiveness, there is a stage at which it needs to efficiently reach real world media too. The problem is that ignoring the traditional role of a comms department means missing out on huge platforms (press, radio, TV) that are followed by millions and have a heft and authority that changes minds. Today you can sometimes see people at demonstrations holding up Avaaz placards to claim its territory and place its name into the event's film coverage.

UNICEF Sweden ran a great campaign whose message was "Likes won't save lives" and asked for donations for vaccinations. They ran four YouTube videos that were seen across 195 countries, 750,000 times in all and generated 10,000 tweets. It served to move supporters into becoming donors. The actual text was, "Like us on Facebook and we will vaccinate zero children against polio," however it was then followed by asking for €4 to save the lives of ten children. This should be a wake-up call to those slacktivists among us lazy enough not to integrate online and real world campaigns, or who don't actually give a donation ourselves.

Many charities make the mistake of hiring people who understand their issues, write well and are articulate, but who have not worked as a journalist or in a similar occupation. It is far easier for a journalist to understand a charity than it is for a charity professional to make the media work for them. Unless you have the mindset and comprehension of a journalist then it is exceedingly hard to put yourself in the shoes of those whom you will be pitching ideas to and you may find that report after report gets binned, but once that barrier is crossed the result can transform the department and the organisation.

Ten tips for an effective communications department

1. Set the strategy and plan the route

Planning and then communicating that plan internally ensures we all know what we should be doing and what others should be doing. Open communications is the hallmark of a confident, successful organisation. The plan should show the communications objectives and how to reach them. It should set out the tasks required over the next few years and so frame the staff requirements now, and in future, as far as possible. From that managers can evaluate staff and work on their roles and relationships. That may involve training, coaching, mentoring and it may even involve redundancy which managers should not shirk from when necessary if they are to build an effective team.

2. Evaluate the campaigns

Here I am talking about media campaigns and any associated activity, for example events. Once objectives are set the evaluation becomes a question of whether they have indeed been reached. They should be both numerical and look at the audience reached – was it the right one? Also, did the communication actually convey what it was supposed to convey? This may be more difficult to evaluate, but the use of questionnaires, surveys and focus groups should help to give a clear picture. If you can't evaluate it then you really don't know if you are wasting your time and that can lead to demotivation and complacency.

3. Hire the right staff

Or rather, hire staff with appropriate experience and knowledge. It is easy to know what you want to say, but another story to convey it in a way that connects effectively with the media you want to reach. Sometimes that is simply a case of hiring a journalist with a good track record, but if someone within your organisation seems to be the right person it may be that they need to spend time being mentored by a journalist or former journalist. Stepping up within an organisation usually requires acquiring a new skill set, whether that is managing staff, taking on board knowledge of a new area or communicating with the media, but each of these hurdles can be surmounted with help.

4. Cover the waterfront

Old media, new media and simply talking to people are all part of a communicator's life and we are living through one of the fastest moving and most exciting times for communications. A department that embraces these changes and new developments, neglecting none, can achieve great breakthroughs as the playing field is levelled out each time a new communication channel opens. Even if you are a one-person department you need not be self-restricting but take up the challenge and look to make early hits when things change because you are not restricted in your role like people in larger departments. Plus you should be able to gain early acceptance for your messages and so get them out there much more quickly than your larger rivals.

5.   Be prepared for a crisis

Inevitably there is a crisis brewing out there somewhere waiting to engulf your organisation and you had better be prepared. Agree a plan with your managers so you know who to call or how to react when the media storm hits, while you are sitting at home having a quiet night in. Make sure this is clear across the organisation, so that everyone knows the procedure and who should talk to the media and who should not. Make sure all staff know that nothing is ever 'off the record', despite what they will be told.

Make sure everyone has the key facts about the charity at their fingertips, literally, perhaps with a small memo with answers to the tough questions like what percentage of your income goes on overheads, how much is your CEO paid, how do you raise your funds and what are your financial reserves?

6. Be prepared for a triumph

When things go well it is tempting to sit back and enjoy the fact your message is trending and your phone won't stop ringing, but thinking about how you can build on this attention and turn a success into something that goes viral is vital. Again planning is essential – do you have your patrons' contact details to hand so you can ask them for a quote and reach their supporters too? Can you leverage this coverage to reach other goals, for example for recruitment or to sell out an event?

7. Test, learn and test again

Love digital media as well as traditional forms and embrace change, but test your ideas, think about the results and improve your communications steadily. Try all new media early on and keep testing. See how your competitors and partners are dealing with changes and improve on their performance. As a sector, I have noticed we are particularly bad at learning from others; we tend to think, "This is the way we do it," when much better models abound if only we looked for them.

8. Integrate your campaigns

It is far better to run fewer campaigns across more media than lots of small ones to limited channels. Once you have synergy working for you and people begin to see the same message a few times they are far more likely to pay attention than if they just hear your message once. Make sure that your different communications are logically connected and make sure your messages, if they are separate, reinforce each other. This is important over time as the campaign evolves and not just at its starting point.

9. Look for unusual outlets

If you have segmented your target audience then think about the media that group uses. For example, regional media is often neglected but may reach them very cost-effectively, magazines they usually read or appropriate radio programmes. If you are unsure then survey that segment separately, learn their demographics and consider how they think and what influences them.

10. Take professional development seriously

Because we are often doing very similar tasks each week for several years it is easy to sink into mere repetition and fail to notice the changes that have affected our profession. We should all be taking part in a form of continuous professional development (CPD) and, as managers, we should ensure our staff are doing likewise. There are many forms of CPD available but simple training in new skills when required is also very beneficial and can often prevent the mistakes people may make when they learn complex tasks by themselves at work.

Be more dog

O2's excellent campaign encouraging everyone to stop being lazy like cats and to be more like dogs, who are engaged and excited by life's possibilities, was a great example of a campaign run across several media from print to TV and into games and YouTube videos. It really engaged with audiences even allowing them to throw Frisbees from their smartphone to their cat on the computer. The basic premise is 'Stop being a zombie, get out there and enjoy life by using O2' (rather than getting a grip on your job and your life). Of course, it would be great to have O2's spend but if a comms department can't spend like O2, it can use its imagination to come up with campaigns that really resonate with the organisation's supporters and potential supporters.

The Scottish Government launched its 'No knives, better lives' campaign with an interesting insight, which was that young men were less likely to carry a knife if they thought about the consequences for their mother if they did. The campaign provided information and support to local organisations fighting knife crime. Much stronger than a 'Don't do it' message, this campaign seeks to inform and deter. Based on research it again uses an imaginative approach which is the hallmark of an effective comms department – much more dog

Here's one last campaign just to show that a great idea and an integrated campaign can live on year after year. 'Movember' was launched in 2003 and is still with us. The campaign, which asks men to grow sponsored moustaches, has raised some £65m and is still going strong, with 1.2m mentions last year on social media. Prostate Cancer UK is one of the top beneficiaries and part of the campaign's brilliance is in using humour to raise funds for a serious condition. It also builds on the bonding of shared experience, with an irreverent pitch that men are responding to, and shows what a great comms department can achieve.

Fortunately charities are steadily increasing the status of their comms departments. Some 20 years ago, 50% of charities had a director of communications and now that figure is 87%, according to CharityComms. This may partly be due to the rise of digital media and a growing acceptance that charities need to be seen online if they are not to become invisible to the next generation of their supporters. Salaries too are on the rise. Hopefully, it is also due to an increasing perception that comms can deliver huge value when properly resourced and respected within the charity.

So, the next time you put your head around the door of your comms department and notice one or more zombies lurking within, it is time for you to instigate change and that change may transform your whole organisation.

6 Zombie finance

One of the most debilitating aspects of working in the third sector is the war between the finance and fundraising departments, which has probably raged on since charities were invented. On the one hand finance departments are there to follow the rules and success for them means ensuring these are not broken. The accounts appear on time and are a correct reflection of the state of the organisation's finances. Money coming in is correctly recorded, as is money being paid out to cover bills, salaries and the rest, and nothing goes astray during this process.

On the other hand, fundraising sees rules as subordinate to actually raising money and if the rules stop money coming in they can be objected to, changed or more likely simply ignored. Taking a risk is natural to fundraising but anathema to finance. The whole character of a great fundraiser is different to that of a great finance officer and in my experience as a CEO and as a consultant that difference makes for a volatile mix.

Sometimes the lack of respect for each other's opinions can have disastrous consequences. I was chatting to the head of finance of a large charity some years ago (let's call him Ted) and asked about the charity's flow of income from its largest branches overseas. Each year these branches were asked to give a percentage of the income they had received a couple of years earlier to the central umbrella organisation. This made it easy for the branch to set this money aside and for the central organisation to know what was coming in, allowing the budget to be set. As a new MBA I was keen to show off my knowledge of international finance and asked about 'selling forward'. Simply put, if you know you will receive $1m in a year's time and need to convert it to pounds to spend, then if you wait a year the currency markets may well have shifted and you only get, say, 80% of the money you were expecting once the dollars are converted to pounds at the new rate. Of course, you might also get more than you expected, but this is unpredictable. To stop this happening you 'sell forward' the dollars, so in a year's time you receive exactly what you expected.

Ted looked rather surprised and said, "We don't do that, it's gambling." It turned out that in recent years the dollar had been steadily strengthening in relation to the pound, and so each year he had more pounds than he expected, which covered any failures in other income streams. "But," I pointed out indignantly, "one year it will go the other way and the organisation will be seriously short of the money it was expecting." Ted wouldn't budge from his position that this was typical of fundraisers wanting to gamble with the organisation's money. And, he added, hadn't his approach proved to be the safe one time and again? The next year the inevitable happened and the organisation was short $1m and a head of finance.

Maybe not your typical zombie but that lack of awareness is frightening from a professional supposedly at the top of their game. More typical of zombie finance departments is the one where, in a rapidly expanding organisation, staff let problems pile up on their desk taking no remedial action until new members leave in droves because they have not heard from the charity and their payments were only processed months after they donated.

The killer zombie comes when the finance department simply can't produce the right figures or produces completely the wrong figures. I worked with an organisation that had once been very large and nationally known but had failed to renew itself, but was now supported by a very elderly contingent of loyal fans who had joined years ago and had no interest in sharing their hobby with a younger generation. Many of the local groups consisted of nearly all elderly women as the men had died.

Despite its decline the organisation retained its complexity from years past including various allied companies and charities with separate accounts, consolidated accounts and a rather obscure ownership structure for some buildings that represented the assets of the main charity. Much of the finance subcommittee's time was taken up by the finance director answering questions like, "This can't be right; you are under-reporting income from our shop on a quarterly basis, and placing it in the wrong charity's account," followed by long explanations about the shop being run by a company, not one of the charities.

The fact was that no one felt they really understood what was going on, the director relied on the finance director as he didn't understand the accounts himself, and the finance director seemed inclined to move things around the accounts to please the subcommittee; always arriving late for the meetings and shuffling his papers, and probably the figures, whilst the committee patiently waited for him to get to the point.

Somewhere at the heart of the organisation a vacuum was opening up which no amount of number juggling could hide. When it was decided to sell one of the buildings, instead of borrowing against it, the charity discovered that it didn't actually own the property. It had been owned by the founder who had passed on years before. He had always talked about it as belonging to the charity but it was legally owned by a separate organisation that had no intention of selling it or giving anything to the charity.

The director had the good sense to change the auditors who had been too close to the finance director and also to appoint a new finance director who discovered that the shop had run at a loss for years. However, it was now too late to do anything about it and the organisation ended up losing nearly all its staff, leaving the director clinging on and longing for retirement.

At the time I too found the accounts baffling. But once the new finance director closed redundant accounts and changed the legal structure into one charity rather than a plethora of charities and companies, the accounts showed a simple and true picture of a small charity that had little income but, once many of the staff had gone, was finally living within its means.

The risks

Once the finances of an organisation become obscure, it is effectively out of control and in danger from a range of risks – not least fraud. Accountants take a mechanical look at the organisation, do not deliver an MOT-type verdict and don't have the overview that a director should bring, so many things can be missed. All they are saying is that the accounts are as accurate as they can ascertain without necessarily going through all the figures.

Simplicity is the key to readable accounts and looking at the movement of figures over three years, not one, will graphically illustrate the direction of travel of the income and expenditure streams. Once when I was helping to merge two organisations I found that certain lines of expenditure were steadily rising year on year, when the number of beneficiaries was falling rapidly each year – it was time to check the bulging stockroom.

Employing staff with the right accounting background, who have a love of numbers and for whom order is at the heart of a great finance department, is the way to go. If the inputting is diligent and timely, the results can be surprisingly informative about the workings of an organisation, and form a proper basis for decision-making.

The monthly accounts are management's key tool for everyday decisions and a good discipline for building up to the annual accounts. If senior managers are looking at the budget and the actual results line by line each month, they can adjust for poor or good performance in time to stop the organisation suffering from unexpected catastrophic failure. Though as John Harvey Jones said, "… the nicest thing about not planning is that failure comes as a complete surprise, rather than being preceded by a period of worry and depression."

Paying the staff on time is the one thing that finance departments tend to get right nearly all the time, as it is immediately apparent if this is not done properly and causes a swift backlash as staff members' mortgages head into arrears. It can be a clear warning signal and if those payments go wrong on a regular basis there are likely to be many more problems around the corner. Not paying suppliers on time, or at all, can be hidden for quite a long time as the bills mount up, but not paying the staff leads to public humiliation. Once people feel the organisation is going under they will jump ship without hesitation.

Managing cash flow so that the bills are paid on time is therefore a key role for any finance department. Flagging up potential problems in advance also prevents poor decision-making by the director or senior management team. If finance works in collaboration with fundraising, the organisation can also plan for occasional large payments and set aside money to invest in development.

Few charities have large reserves and three to six months is probably typical. For some with possibly much greater periodic calls on their purse it may be necessary to carry several months' reserves ring-fenced against the inevitable demand. If the charity carries too much reserve, then it will have a hard time fundraising from grant-makers or wealthy donors, both of whom are likely to see the accounts and to notice any large sums sitting idle. The greatest security for any charity is not to have oodles of money in the bank but to have a well-funded development programme with the whole organisation behind it.

Finance directors can be invaluable in advising managers about key strategic decisions but they need to know and understand the pattern of income and expenditure over a number of years. With a poor grasp of the figures, or simply a misunderstanding, the advice is likely to lead to bad decisions with major repercussions. Timidity may be the typical finance director's abiding sin, as their profession is quite rightly cautious, but any growing organisation seeking to improve the lives of many more of its beneficiaries will need to have an entrepreneurial outlook and to take some risks. During critical times any advice coming from finance may need to be tempered by a look at what the numbers actually say, rather than the officer's interpretation of them.

Finance departments are responsible for many compliance issues such as tax and the financial side of employment, as well as various other statutory and legal requirements. Once the zombies have gathered in finance these are the first areas to go haywire, often gradually as returns are made late, numbers made up and figures shuffled around to hide ineptitude. These are all key issues that will seriously damage an organisation if they go wrong and are not dealt with promptly. Once the relevant authorities investigate they will then bill for back-tax with interest, and possibly a host of other things that have been neglected including the dreaded VAT payments. Death and taxes may be the only certain things in life and for an organisation the act of not paying tax can be followed closely by its financial death.

Listing everything that might go wrong in a finance department could take up the rest of this chapter so let's look on the bright side at the brilliance of a great department that gives helpful advice and plays an active part in key decisions. This is never truer than when the budgets are drawn up as that really sets the scene for all parts of the organisation to move forward with enough staff and other resources. Equally when a charity is in decline and laying off staff and losing support a great finance department will be invaluable in helping senior managers to scale back staff and other expenditure, showing where savings can be made and temporary solutions adopted if required.

All this points to the key role of a head of finance and the imagination required for them to play a significant role in the life of the organisation. This role is about far more than making sure the right numbers are in the right place. It is about having a grasp of strategy for the whole organisation over a number of years.

Ten ways to stop zombies taking over your finance department

1. You really, really have to understand the finances yourself. It is not that hard and there are many courses out there to help you read a balance sheet and even to prepare one to trial balance stage. You

don't need to pass an accountancy degree; basic knowledge is your prime protection, without which you are in the hands of any zombie who thinks they have a talent for numbers. We all learn quickly on the job, but it is one thing to pick up budgeting, which is pretty straightforward (and really up to those compiling the budgets), but quite another to read the accounts in a way that will give you deep insights into your financial flow.

2. Be curious and ask questions. If you get into that habit in relation to any set of figures then when it really counts you will be asking the right questions. Chat to the accountants too especially the ones in a huddle tutting over your books. Yes, those odd amounts, however small, that don't add up correctly, are important. It may be that larger numbers have been moved around to hide something and those small numbers are the ones that someone couldn't quite shove under the carpet in time. If you ask the obvious questions at the outset so that you understand what is in front of you then you gain a sound basis for moving on to ask more difficult questions, especially about the figures that may not be in front of you.

3. Employing the right people in the first place, using the recruitment methods outlined earlier, is an obvious point and the interviews I like best are those where the candidate also has some practical exercises to do.

"Please take five minutes to read these accounts and describe the organisation to us," can be very revealing, as can a numerical exercise of the "Why don't these figures add up?" variety. I am always surprised at the number of people with great CVs who just can't carry out basic tasks in their supposed profession.

4. Cash flow is the lifeblood of an organisation and the quickest way for life to become extinct is when the cash flow dries up. Yes, you may be owed very large sums but they are no good to you sitting in someone else's bank account. The prompt collection of money owed and the regular chasing for those payments are crucial. In many charities this may be the membership fees which, if based on monthly direct debits, will flow freely into your account. However, when people lapse they need to be reminded and more than once. If many of your payments come in the form of large government grants then ensure you know when they are due to arrive and just how secure they are, especially in times of austerity or recession. If you have cash flow problems you may need to stagger your own payments to suppliers and this should not be left to finance alone. They are unlikely to understand the effect of keeping certain people waiting for money.

5. Keep a check that the accounts are produced on time and sent to the Charity Commission where many

people will look at them. Their website shows how diligent an organisation is in returning its accounts on time. A large gift may well pass you by if the accounts are repeatedly delayed. Any potential donor will check with the Charity Commission online and if there are delays this signals poor financial control. Getting the accounts out close to the year end is a good discipline and will also greatly improve your chance of grant funds as most grant-makers expect to see recently signed accounts.

6. Paying your taxes on time saves fines and enquiries. It also saves having an overly optimistic idea of the available income. Don't forget to ask, "Where are we on tax and VAT?" In a busy life it is easy to assume finance is beavering away comfortably but we are all human and things get missed – but they certainly get missed a lot less often if someone is enquiring about them.

7. Do we ever look at investments? Large charities often have a certain number of investments and old charities often have a large amount, but over time the performance changes and it helps to check on them regularly. Warren Buffet advises buying shares in solid household name companies and keeping them for twenty years. You may not be able to take the long view and some share prices will fall permanently as new players using new technology and the like steal their

market. Don't put all your eggs in one basket. In 2004, Amaranth Advisors bought heavily into natural gas and made $1 billion, but went bankrupt the following year losing over $5 billion – one of the biggest losses ever.

8. In larger organisations the role of financial oversight may extend to cover the various parts of the organisation that both spend and raise money. Ensuring that these units are not both exceeding their expenditure and failing to draw in adequate income may be the responsibility of the finance department, or the CEO, but it needs to be clear whose task it is. And when things do go wrong there should be a clear policy on how to put them right.

In the words of The King's Fund talking about the NHS:

"The case for having a well-understood, transparent and automatic regime for dealing with financial failure is clear. First, it should return a struggling organisation to financial good health or find an alternative way to provide services to patients. Second, its existence should provide incentives to other organisations not to fall into similar financial difficulties and thus help to improve NHS efficiency more widely. Without such a system there is a danger that the NHS is pushed into providing 'bail-outs' that prop up inefficient services and blunt incentives for efficiency."

9. We are in a period of exceptionally low interest payments and organisations that have been tempted to borrow heavily will need to repay or service those debts at a significantly higher rate in the years to come. This interest rate shock should come as no surprise and early repayment is a virtue best not ignored.

10. Finally, let's be clear that moral failure comes before financial collapses. There is a kind of hubris that says, "I know best and no one else is smart enough to understand or find out what I am doing". This attitude coupled with a lack of common sense can pervade any department especially those dealing with a fairly esoteric subject like finance. Be on your guard because we can all fail to supervise properly.

The best academic work on this is: 'Why moral failures precede financial crises', David Weitzner and James Darroch (2009), *Critical perspectives on international business*, Volume 5. Issue 1/2, pp.6–13.

Learning points

Let's take three key points out of all this. The first is that the finance department can enrich any organisation's decision-making if it is well run. Running a finance department takes more than an aptitude with numbers and requires management skills to ensure that all the staff are performing at a high level as well as an understanding of the whole organisation including its appetite for risk. Investment drives forward growth and a positive but judicious input into the budget for the next few years can give exceptional security through efficient and effective development.

Secondly, prudence is essential to avoid long-term problems. Though that should not hamper judicious investment in income-generation, it should guard against over-optimistic estimations of income or underestimation of expenditure on any project under debate.

Thirdly, finance staff can cause immense harm to an organisation. Conversely their knowledge, honesty and integrity can be central to the survival and prosperity of the whole organisation. To give a simple example many charities collect Gift Aid from the government (which occurs when a donor who is also a taxpayer makes a donation and signs a Gift Aid form). The charity can then reclaim the tax that donor has paid (it gets more complicated with higher-rate taxpayers and gifts of shares and the like but we will ignore that for now) and the finance department collects the money. The latter is often a task that zombie finance departments put off for extraordinary lengths of time, so damaging the cash flow of the organisation.

And remember the signed accounts are not the whole story: look at Enron, look at Kids Company.

What does the finance department do?

The key roles of a finance department are:

1. Keeping the books.

These days we all work on computers and keeping the spreadsheets might be a more appropriate heading, though we still talk about using ledgers. Simply put, the books record money coming in and money going out in a timely fashion. So finance is responsible for paying the invoices that come in and receiving donations. The latter means it is often also responsible for thanking donors and issuing welcome packs. The speed with which donors receive such information is the speed and measure of efficiency that they perceive the organisation to employ in the field, so it is essential to building long-term support that these functions are carried out efficiently.

2. Setting out the balance sheet and profit and loss (P&L) account.

Periodically the books are used to create a view of the organisation's finances, for example at the end of the financial year. A trial balance is set up to show the assets and liabilities of the organisation in balance. Then the income and expenditure are added together to create the P&L account. This is the key annual documentation which is approved (or not) by the auditors and signed off by the board of trustees. It is, however, a historical record and often nearly a year old by the time it has been signed off and distributed, so on its own it is hardly an adequate check on the finances.

3. Providing management information.

This is the opportunity for finance to play its part in the key decisions of the organisation and to ensure they are made in a way that will not jeopardise the organisation's future. For example, the timing of financial expenditure may be crucial and may not be something of which senior managers are normally aware. The monthly accounts are the other significant piece of management information without which the organisation is flying blind into the future.

4. Management of wages and pensions.

From the staff's point of view this is the most important function of any finance department and it is a quick litmus test of its professionalism to have the wages posted accurately and on time. The wages, however, must not be determined by the finance department on purely financial grounds. They are a key motivator or demotivator and should require a shared decision by senior management, or at times a decision by the director and chair of the board.

5. Securing funding.

In a corporate structure the finance department is responsible for raising funds such as bank loans or other borrowings, and for paying the resulting interest. In charities the fundraising department is responsible for bringing in the money set out in the budget. The finance department should definitely not be in charge of the fundraising department. The finance department is also responsible for handling any reserves which may be placed on the money market or wherever is deemed suitable. It will also be responsible for any borrowing and the setting up of an overdraft facility.

Finance is such a clear-cut thing with definite rules that one would think it was the least likely part of an organisation to go wrong, but it is run and policed by fallible humans just like all the other departments. Sometimes a charity, perhaps more so than a commercial organisation, has people who tend to be baffled by the books and this means that oversight may be lacking. Any department that feels it is ignored can begin to develop practices which are convenient for the people managing the department but may not be advisable in the long run. When there is someone not pulling their weight, or acting inadvisably, it is easy to let it go for so long that it becomes a huge problem and thus a breeding ground for zombies.

Problems can come from simple things like not having two people open the post. So, if a donor posts a large cash sum (and they do) and it doesn't arrive, then no one knows if it was ever posted or went missing and perhaps unjust suspicion may fall on the post-opener; whereas with two people there is at least a modicum of backup. There is always a reason for odd behaviour and I have seen it go unscrutinised to devastating effect. If a certain volunteer always arrives in finance on Thursdays and insists on entering the takings from the same event themselves when there are plenty of other people to do it, ask yourself why. Thoughtful checks are vitally important and without them those small problems can grow until we look at the draft accounts and go, "OMG is that all we have in the bank!"

Chinese walls – Chinese whispers

Some organisations like Friends of the Earth and Amnesty have at least two basic legal entities: one the campaigning body and a charitable arm too, with possibly another separate company to run shops or other trading activities with the profits deeded back to the charity or campaigning group.

All the parts of the enterprise are very clearly financially and legally separate. The charity cannot simply give the trading company money as that is not a charitable purpose and a charity must be wholly charitable. Neither can the charity give funds to the campaigning wing of an organisation if again that is not a charitable activity. The trustees of the charity can make whatever decision they so choose as an independent body and they need not obey any other part of the organisation.

It is quite acceptable for the finances of all these organisations to be run by the same finance department, but there has to be a clear separation of the flow of funds and the roles of the finance employees. The people whose wages are charged to, say, the charity must be only those who worked for the charity, though someone may spend two days a week on one entity and three on another. In this case their time can be paid for by splitting the cost proportionately between the various entities.

All this can prove to be a minefield when zombie staff wander from one desk to another and help themselves to work. So, not only does the finance department need to fully understand the legal and technical requirements, but also the fine detail of which staff are working on which account and how their time is allocated. The floor space also becomes important as that may also be charged across as rent from one part of the organisation to another.

Occasionally, where so called 'political' campaigning is the *raison d'être* of the organisation, the charity may take a back seat, with little regard to who the trustees are until a fundraising programme proves very successful and the charity becomes very wealthy, perhaps even more so than the original organisation. I have seen this happen with a very successful door-to-door operation, when the direct debits began stacking up year after year, and the brainwave of putting wealthy donors in as trustees no longer seemed such a great idea – unless you were one of the wealthy donors. Once these donors were aware of their independence and position of power they began to decide exactly which piece of research the charity would pay for and just what educational projects would be funded. This didn't go down well with the campaigners who had quite different ideas and wanted the research to give them ammunition for campaigning not just to meet the trustees' perceived educational needs. This was perhaps a case where sleeping zombies refused to remain lying down and rose to create their own kind of well-meant havoc.

Post script: local groups

Local groups can breed a whole new category of zombies with rather limited horizons and a distinctly short-sighted approach to finance. One of our clients had grown from a robust local group structure, but wasn't quite aware how robust until they learned that the local groups together had over £1m in their bank accounts waiting for a rainy day in their own town. The news that the central organisation had a serious cash flow problem and needed help fell on deaf ears, as the local groups felt that they were certainly not going to pay for the central organisation profligacy from their prudent savings, and harsh words were exchanged.

The central organisation then decided to institute back-to-back banking whereby in January each year the bank would sweep through all the local group accounts and take out any surplus apart from about three months' expenditure. The organisation explained how it could get an excellent deal by all the groups moving to one bank and the local groups explained they got a very good deal by staying exactly where they were.

Wars between local groups and central offices are frequent and not pretty. In this case the local groups had the right to choose one third of the council members from their local group membership, and at the next AGM they used their votes and influence to block any attempt to push through financial reform. Though they nominally held less than fifty per cent of the votes, they were used to exerting their influence by lobbying the other council members, talking at length to try and get things dropped off the agenda and doing deals with interest groups to ensure they had a majority when the time came. I doubt they had had that much fun in years.

Case study – Kids Company

At its height Kids Company was the 'go to' children's charity for three political administrations: New Labour, the Coalition and then the Conservatives on their own. Led by its charismatic director, Camila Batmanghelidjh, CBE, who had the ability to impress all who listened to her, the charity grew exponentially. Originally it asked for professional staff to be on loan from local authorities, which gave it a sound professional base, and as the work grew it raised increasingly large sums until its turnover in 2013 was some £23 million. David Cameron's Big Society rhetoric found a home in Kids Company, pleased that it reached kids that local authorities did not seem to be good at helping.

Begun in 1996 as a drop-in centre, Kids Company worked with children from some of the most disadvantaged families in England, principally in the London boroughs of Lambeth and Southwark, and later in Bristol. It refused to turn any child away and the numbers which it helped rose from 14,000 in 2009 to 36,000 (including young people and families) in 2013. Local authorities have a legal duty to safeguard vulnerable children in their area and Kids Company was seen to work effectively with the most difficult children.

It suddenly closed its doors in August 2015, having effectively run out of funds, and used part of the final tranche of £3m from the Government to pay its last wages. Shortly before it closed, a potential donor of another £3m pulled out, citing a forthcoming police investigation.

So, why had this amazing charity with its income in the millions of pounds, beloved of prime ministers, a host of celebrities and (until close to the end) an adoring media, closed so abruptly? The answer in part lies in the fact they never turned a child away, so however much they raised there was always more to do. Year after year, the charity failed to put away adequate reserves and that built the proverbial house of cards. In 2009 they were £127,000 in debt followed by a build-up the next year towards three months' reserves but in later years this too disappeared.

The trustees whose responsibility it was to oversee the finances were repeatedly warned that the reserves were inadequate for that size of organisation. The accounts lodged with the Charity Commission clearly noted the problem. This is where a zombie board's lack of ability to act decisively at the right time can prove fatal. The ability of the CEO to pull the chestnuts out of the fire year after year does not mean that financial prudence can be overlooked. At a time of volatile financial change adequate reserves become a necessity to guard against a downturn.

Kids Company's chair of the board was Alan Yentob, the BBC's creative director, who was there almost from the beginning seeing its expansion from under a railway arch to the establishment of its centres in London, Bristol and Liverpool. Although Kids Company's own financial directors advised building up adequate reserves (and occasionally resigned in protest) this never happened and a media storm erupted over the closure, engulfing both the chair and the CEO.

Kids Company proved to be a very sad case but illustrative of the need to follow professional advice at all levels and not become zombified by any apparent suspension of the laws of finance and fundraising.

7 Zombies in the field

Some years ago, courtesy of Oxfam, I was staring down a newly built well in Zimbabwe wondering why it was full of frogs and considering their chances of being kissed, which weren't very high. And it struck me that frogs live in open wells – always have, always will – and just because the well was freshly dug to provide a village with drinking water didn't mean the frogs would respectfully stay away. Much worse was the carelessness of another NGO that built a well where the village headman instructed and were horrified when he then charged villagers to use the well because it was built on his land. Work in the field is complex and demands a lot of local knowledge that isn't just about the project, or the beneficiaries' problems, but about the whole environment in which such problems arise.

A Christian organisation in Zimbabwe was helping small cooperative farmers to breed chickens for eggs provided they held regular prayer meetings, which they did rather sheepishly. As communist ex-combatants they had all heard the sayings that the white man came with priests in front of him and guns behind. Or similarly that when they closed their eyes to pray the land was in their hands, and the Bible in the white man's hands, but after they had prayed they opened their eyes and the Bible was in their hands and their land was in the hands of the white man. Unfortunately, despite much help and financial advice with the chicken project, the fact that the charity created a lot of chicken farms meant that the market was flooded with eggs and the farms went under. What happened to the Bibles? I have no idea.

If fishermen are ripped off by middlemen who pay them half what they should get for their catch, then doubling their catch may only mean the middlemen pay them a quarter of what it is worth and you have only enriched the middlemen. Doubling the catch may endanger the fish stock and also attract more fishermen, which may mean the price of fish falls anyway as the market becomes glutted with fish. And this speeds up the demise of the fish stock. Hiring lawyers to defend the fishermen may work but then further up the chain the retailers may drop the price, impoverishing both the middlemen and the fishermen.

This is not to say there is no hope. Years of successful development by brilliant NGOs combined with massive debt relief from the Jubilee 2000 campaign, and more recently Chinese government investment in infrastructure, mineral extraction and manufacturing, has begun to transform Africa. I saw this recently in Uganda where the annual growth rate was close to 5%. Ugandan Government economic reforms and a smart handling of the 2008 downturn have also played their part. Worldwide, concentrated work on the millennium development goals has seen significant improvements especially in the deaths of children under five years of age, the primary education of girls in southern Asia and the number of people globally living on less than $1.25 a day. These are truly astonishing achievements considering the scale of the problems.

Evaluate and be damned

If it is difficult in the field overseas it is also difficult at home. When taking on a client I simply divide their annual income by the number of people they have helped each year to see how cost-effective their work appears to potential donors. Sometimes it would appear much cheaper to give the beneficiaries the cash to spend themselves but then there would be no more income in future years. And why should anyone give in the absence of proper asks and professional fundraisers?

One client was doing an amazing job with people who were very difficult to help, but was finding it hard to raise money because no one really believed they could be successful. The charity also believed that they could not evaluate their work because it was so complex. Even though they did a good job it was still possible that the beneficiary was worse off than before, though not as badly off as they would have been if the charity had not intervened. The truth here is that the charity workers, though experts in their own field, were not professional about monitoring and evaluation, which is evolving into a professional field of its own. If you are doing great work it can always be evaluated, and any deterioration in those you are trying to help can be accounted for and certainly should not be deemed a failure if it really is a success.

The therapists in one organisation I worked with were a case in point. The clinicians I talked to simply didn't believe that their work could be evaluated. Strange then that when they were asked to describe how they talked to their clients it became obvious that the first thing they did was to evaluate each client at the start of the session by asking a series of pertinent questions.

UN missions occasionally cause serious problems in the field because they may be there to respond to an emergency and have put someone in charge that just doesn't think about their work in the critical way they need to when working in a much poorer country. A zombie in charge, or just in contact with the people they should be helping, is then a serious liability and their actions can be fatal. The UN contingent that responded to the Haiti earthquake, for example, which was accused of contaminating water upstream of people's drinking water. Or the abuse by UN soldiers in several conflict zones including the Democratic Republic of Congo (DRC). Leaders in the field need to be selected with care and briefed by the right people before they leave their home base fully aware of the consequences of poor decision-making.

Managing field staff, especially those who have been in the field for a long time and are well respected back home, is not easy when it comes to evaluating their work and challenging poor practice. Complacency can creep in when field staff live abroad for many years and home-country staff change frequently as this makes it hard to get a real grip on performance. The best staff can turn into zombies if they fail to adapt to new conditions or if they feel that their managers do not appreciate what they do. If these staff do not have respect for their manager it will become evident when the manager's request for that extra trip to a project far from the capital is put off when the tropical fish tank needs a clean or any other trivial reason.

Field staff or field officers may be rather grand names for staff who work in the home country. For staff working in the regions far from head office or for those who deal directly with beneficiaries on a daily basis the same problems arise of managing people over distance and keeping them motivated and up to date in their thinking.

What can go wrong probably will go wrong

Zombies in the field can bring an organisation to its knees with remarkable rapidity. With twenty-four-hour news coverage from around the world and charity staff held to high standards by the media, any significant lapse may trigger an avalanche of bad news, even if the original accusation is an exaggeration or simply unproven. A staff member who has ceased to be effective and lets things slide can cause a local problem that becomes a regional one and then a national and international headache for the organisation. It is much worse if staff actually cause harm by taking advantage of those with whom they are working, so careful recruitment and meticulous monitoring of their work is vital for the short term and the long term.

Weak decisions and poor management practice at local level undermine the promises made to the donors, be they individuals, institutions or companies. Often a field officer will work through a network of local charities or NGOs and it is rarely practical to give them the funds for their operations and walk away. The crucial element is always how their work impacts on the people they are trying to help over a long period of time. Of course, we know that this work is difficult, often in appalling conditions, and fraught with difficulty and complexity. When things go wrong, prompt reporting and quick action to correct the problem is vital in preventing a large-scale difficulty emerging. In such cases it is vital to have effective monitoring and professional oversight, and to be able to accurately describe to concerned media just what steps are being taken.

Once others in the organisation realise that someone has ceased to bother to perform it is twice as hard to hold them to account, as the zombie will begin to infect others. Local organisations that know they are not monitored will have much less incentive to fight bribery and corruption, and they may even turn a blind eye to things that would cause outrage among donors and the media.

When we are dealing with work in the home country the same thing applies: it is not that a staff member is failing to keep up with the paperwork, or not turning up for all the meetings they should; it is the effect their behaviour has on those they are trying to help, and its ability to grow into a national scandal all too quickly, that may be the problem. The closer that staff are to the beneficiaries, the more the media can raise moral indignation over their behaviour and this in turn can place all charities under suspicion for a time.

It is however much harder to deal with people who, whilst they may not be very good or effective, are not obviously causing any immediate harm. This is the real challenge of zombies, as they potter on ineffectually and the problems grow and multiply till managers are faced with a very serious situation and have to take far more drastic action than they may have wanted. The question is: could the situation have been avoided if they had taken action when it was a small problem requiring little attention? Perhaps that's the time for some inspiring behaviour to remotivate staff or possibly to organise a rapid changeover of staff.

A disaster is a prime cause for concern whether it is an earthquake, flood or famine, as a lot of people may be drafted in at short notice and without the level of training or sensitisation that the situation really requires. Cultural sensitivity is paramount as culture can override what we might regard as common sense and make interventions null and void in quick time. Yet it is one of the hardest things to put across because we all think our culture is the right way to do things and the temptation to impose it is very strong, especially in an emergency when it is obvious quick action and fast reactions are required.

The whole nature of the intervention may be fraught with difficulty. Should we import food that will impoverish local suppliers, and what sort of food is acceptable and will be eaten? Whose land do we save first and whose land do we let go in the face of flood or fire? What protection should we give to refugees and for how long? These decisions are often taken far from the emergency itself and only prompt, accurate feedback may avert compounding the disaster. This means that the people on the ground should be highly trained and their training refreshed, as is the case with all the major charities.

On a completely different tack, we often have scruples about testing and research on animals, and for a long time cancer charities seemed to be inflicting a lot of pain on animals without producing any breakthroughs in cancer treatment. The situation has now improved considerably as cancer treatments become increasingly more effective, but this kind of moral dilemma requires a high level of emotional maturity and political awareness, wherever in the organisation decisions are made and especially in the field of research.

The zombie tendency here is to be half-asleep on the job and not realise the implications of the organisation's work for the wider public, however bad that would be. However, it is the lack of intellectual inquisitiveness and a moral compass that prevents an organisation establishing how the everyday work and public perceptions of that work might interact. When this problem exists among the managers of the organisation it is hard for junior staff to question what might be a very large programme. This may force them to become whistle-blowers rather than flagging the issues internally. An early warning of problems is always preferable to late whistle-blowing which might expose serious errors and may reach the media. A charity's culture should always be to welcome an individual highlighting issues rather than feeling under attack. Many examples from the corporate and political world show how difficult this is in practice and how late in the day this kind of thinking has been in emerging.

For us, the symbolic donning of a white coat by operational staff makes it easy not to question 'the expert', but that is exactly what may be needed when moral decisions are required rather than the blind acceptance of the negative side of attaining an organisational goal.

One of the best books on work in the field is Oxfam's excellent *Field Director's Manual*, which runs to 512 pages and is available from Amazon. Oxfam bases its fieldwork on the premise that the best action in the field is the development of people and not necessarily the delivery of equipment, for example. It covers the involvement of local communities and the need to be sensitive to local societal and cultural norms.

Ten things not to forget

1. The first key area is the preparation of staff before they enter the field, whether this is overseas or in the home country. This must of course include cultural and social sensitisation as well as more practical training which should have a healthy dose of evaluation and monitoring included. This is not just because the donors demand it but because it helps the field officers think clearly about what they are doing and why they are doing it. This in turn leads to reporting back as things change, and they nearly always change over time. Field officers may have lived

in-country for many years or even all their life but that doesn't mean they don't need training and the lessons that come from taking a critical look at a country from the outside.

2. The further from HQ any operative works the more important is their management especially motivation and a respite from the stresses of working in difficult situations with very difficult people. Training and socialising back in the home country become a necessity to reconnect with the organisation, the other staff and most importantly, the mission. Management should not be confined to inspecting the work or walking round the projects but it should look at the needs of the staff whether these are for knowledge, perspective or psychologically for support, motivation and praise.

3. Length of time in the field and home visits become critical factors to avoiding burnout and a zombie-like existence. This applies not just to the total number of years an expat may work overseas but the whole pattern of their time in field, time off, time spent training and the like. This is equally important if the field officer is a local hire. The question for them is one of time in the field, time off (perhaps away from the area where the work takes place) and time in the organisation's home country, perhaps with their family.

4. All our skills need updating regularly and work methods and practices need improving from time to time. Field officers can easily become over-involved, especially when they are bringing succour to those in real need, and it may be hard for them to pull back and take a broader view. New techniques can be perceived to trash all the work that has gone before and their introduction should be approached with sensitivity. The words, "I haven't got time for this," may be a literal expression and the subject may need to be introduced later, but it may also signify that the person has become over-involved and needs to pull back in order to recuperate and gain a fresh perspective.

5. Career paths affect us all and though progression from the field may not be easy, with staff feeling they are out of the spotlight, local staff should not be forgotten during recruitment, as they have very practical experience to bring to any new role. Part of the desire for a new position may be that the situation has changed since they were first employed. This can be due to currency exchange movements making their pay worth less locally, or political instability making their posts less secure, or the work may have settled down to be less interesting or, on the other hand, perhaps far more challenging.

6. Don't wait for the performance review before commenting on perceived problems in staff behaviour.

And do be careful to base your comments on observed behaviour rather than on your guesses or intuition about that person. Listen to the answer and don't assume you are completely right about their behaviour; so much changes from day to day in the field compared to the home office and staff have to adapt to those changes, sometimes making it impossible to stick to previously agreed courses of action. A quick and neutral word early on makes a lot of difference, before attitudes and opinions harden on both sides.

7.   Recognition is important too and the further you are from the centre, the harder it may be to feel fully valued and properly rewarded for your work. This makes it easier for field staff to lose interest, passion and belief in what they are doing. Simple recognition of their value, honestly expressed, is a great motivator as well as the more usual forms of recognition and reward such as salary increases, bonuses or formal awards for achievement or long service. It should not be difficult to establish an appropriate system of recognition, for field staff especially, so that there is a regular process for ensuring that they know their work and personal effort is appreciated.

8.   It is all too easy to look at field staff out of context, but it is highly likely that there are other organisations that you can benchmark your progress against. This can lead to better practice but also to a more accurate

evaluation of staff, who may be doing far better, or far worse, than other staff in the field working for different organisations. Talking to beneficiaries, or the agencies through which services are delivered, can be especially revealing as they may have a totally different take from you on the work in which your organisation is engaged.

9. Staff rarely perform badly for no reason. Look at their immediate managers and their personal circumstances. You may be able to turn the situation around by bringing out unseen problems and dealing with them rather than dealing directly with the problematic behaviour. Of course, some breaches of discipline are so egregious that the staff responsible have to be dismissed, but it is always valuable to look at why they occurred and to see if there isn't a deeper problem that needs correcting.

10. Lastly, don't forget your own humanity. The field is where your organisation makes a difference to peoples' lives (or the environment) and insisting on company policy at all costs can be inhuman. Your field staff may have very good reason for not filling in forms, or being in the wrong part of the country at the wrong time, or even for taking decisions that in theory they do not have the permission to take. The watchword may be, what exactly is the effect of their actions on the beneficiaries?

Summary

The worst thing about zombies in the field is that they can go undetected for a long time until the situation finally blows up in your face with a damaging monstering of your organisation or staff by the media. Problems like this also point to other problems higher up the chain of command because somewhere, a manager or two are not doing their duty and are not managing their staff closely enough to understand the situation, or more frequently are afraid to tackle the problem and discipline the guilty party. Sometimes the zombie's manager is just waiting for the problem to go away and the person to move, retire or expire. Unfortunately the zombie doesn't see it like that and is quite happy to sit tight, drawing a salary and doing their job as badly as ever or, as they might perceive it, as brilliantly as they always have.

The introduction to this chapter looked at some examples. Compared with office zombies, those in the field can be more varied and harder to detect. The distances involved can mean that supervision is not close and the dependency of the beneficiaries, who may be vulnerable and even dependent on the field office, may be reluctant to report them. Sometimes this is simply because they are not aware that the staff behaviour is not up to scratch.

The key management metric is often the amount and quality of contact, both personal and by email, phone and Skype, though the latter are not substitutes for actually being with people on the ground and talking to those with whom they deal. Emotions are revealed in the face, so email and the telephone, whilst providing useful information, are just not as good as face-to-face interaction (or even Skyping) for detecting underlying problems. And quality contact of this sort takes time and cannot be rushed if a problem is to be detected and adequately addressed.

Monitoring and evaluation reports are extremely useful in looking at the work accomplished in the field and its effect but we should remember the problems that clothing manufacturers have encountered in trying to ensure that the factories in poor countries that produce their garments are run ethically. They started by insisting on certain standards and agreeing inspection visits. Naturally the sites were fine when the inspectors called. Then the companies tried inspecting at random times but the local inspectors were bribed to turn a blind eye and eventually they used their own inspectors whom they controlled to carry out random inspections. Each change of tack took some time and was often driven by investigative journalists checking to see if the problems still remained. Even now this is still a minefield where companies must tread lightly if they go there at all.

If keeping up standards is hard for rich multinationals who seriously want to avoid a bad press, then think how much harder is it for small-scale NGOs that lack the multinationals' financial clout and fear the ever-present threat of bad publicity.

Nike: a case study

Of course, a major US manufacturer is not the same as an international NGO managing its staff in the field, or monitoring its own activities; but Nike provides a very useful study of the difficulties that arise in the whole process. Consider that the factory owners and local organisations handling funds on behalf of international NGOs are in a rather similar position.

Nike is a classic case of a company that relied on not just the quality of the clothes and shoes it produced in China and Vietnam, but also on its image to sell its products. It does not manufacture its own goods but designs and markets the products. Its image was dented severely when their factories were described in 1997 as sweatshops where basic human rights were abused. Though Nike claimed that this applied to a very small number of factories, and only a few individual cases within those factories, the stories spread so fast that its all-important image was in trouble around the world.

Nike's response was to form a code of practice for the relevant factories but the initial code was attacked by

American unions and had to be reworked. For example it set a minimum age of sixteen for clothing workers in the factories but did not restrict the age in those countries where it was legally permissible to work at fourteen. The lack of a right to organise and the right to a minimum wage were also questioned, and it was pointed out that Coca-Cola, Pepsi, Goodyear and Gillette all had better arrangements over the minimum wage. One problem was that in many countries the legal minimum wage is set very low precisely to attract foreign companies.

Nike also joined the Apparel Industry Partnership (AIP), set up in October 1996 by the Clinton administration, which brought together representatives of clothing manufacturers, unions and human rights groups. AIP developed several standards which were agreed, challenged and revised over subsequent years.

AIP's 'Principles of Monitoring' in April 1997 were signed by Nike but were criticised because they allowed factories to use their own auditors and firms already contracted to them, which created a conflict of interest. The agreement also allowed for only 10% of the factories to be inspected initially followed by only 5% and these would be designated by the companies, which would release the findings themselves, not through independent inspectors.

Nike was accused of only joining AIP to look good and then using its presence there to stall real improvements for workers; but by October 1998 Nike had made significant steps forward. The Interfaith Centre on Corporate Responsibility (ICCR) looked at Nike's factories in China, Vietnam and Indonesia and found that considerable progress had been made. Ventilation was good, overtime had been cut back (workers had previously worked sixty to eighty hours a week for long periods) and in general, health and safety had improved. The processes in these factories often used toxic chemicals from which the workers were now better protected. The 'no talk' rule which prevented workers from speaking whilst they worked was also ended, and where factories were found to be wanting, Nike was implementing appropriate changes.

In January 1999, Nike then shot itself in the foot when its Vice-President Joseph Ha wrote to the Vietnamese government saying that the human rights organisations, and local activists, had political reasons for targeting Nike and were aiming to overthrow the government by creating a democracy in Vietnam. Once this became known, Nike issued a statement to say the statement was only Ha's personal opinion; but it was too late to stop the feeling that Nike had never been that serious about reform and that the people at the top felt they had never done anything wrong apart from being caught in the media searchlight. The real fear was that Nike would backslide as soon as the media attention shifted away.

Fast-forward to 2011 by which time factory inspection had become big business and many organisations were in the game of inspecting thousands of factories to ensure they met the stringent conditions that the companies had set for the factories producing their garments. The trouble was that the companies wanted to bring down the cost of inspection, turning a specialised profession into a commodity and trying to pay as little as $1,000 for each factory inspected, which meant that the operation became a box-ticking exercise and there was no time to talk to workers off-site and investigate thoroughly.

In Guangdong, China, a Walmart-certified factory was due to face inspection and had theoretically produced a range of pet clothing items for Christmas to be sold in Walmart stores in the US. The items had not, however, been produced at the factory but had been produced elsewhere and the factory was disguised to make it look as if they had been produced there. This fooled the inspectors but when the goods were sold in the US there were a large number of complaints about their quality. Reindeer suits and Mrs Claus dresses for dogs may be a million miles away from an NGO's normal remit, but the workers' conditions and the problems of process-monitoring and evaluation are certainly not.

The conclusion here is that we can be sure that the factories are fit for workers only when those workers can organise legitimately and are able to object to illegal conditions that violate their agreements with multinationals and human rights standards.

The conclusion with regard to zombie management is to avoid complacency when you think you have a good system, but keep checking for flaws, because today you may not have the world's press on your doorstep keeping you on your toes, but you just might tomorrow. Indeed exactly that happened in the UK in 2016 when the press vilified the management of some fundraising techniques and the resultant sharp practices.

There are simple things you can do to keep staff working remotely both happy and productive. You may not be able to see what they are doing but you can evaluate their work through setting objectives with a schedule to meet them. This means that you have regular feedback and you know the tasks have been accomplished when they should have been, even if you haven't actually witnessed them taking place yourself. As a manager it may be hard to get used to seeing the results but not the work that went into them, but you are paying for the results not the appearance of work. This means that the content of the objectives needs agreeing when the worker starts, and any changes very close to a renewal of contract should be handled delicately rather than being imposed without discussion.

'Communication, communication, communication' is the mantra for those who work in the field. It is good for managers to set times when their remote staff should report (and the content of those reports) as well as managers being available at certain times in the week, so that ideas or problems can be brought up close to when they occur. Establishing the primary tool of communication is useful whether it is phone, email, Skype or another tool. A simple rule of thumb is if there has been no communication for a week, just call for a chat. When you are far from the office you miss the tea and coffee breaks when workers chat informally and any process that replaces that, albeit in part, is to be welcomed.

Maximise the time you do meet face to face and make sure that this time involves a full discussion of the current and future tasks. It also makes a lot of sense to take time to talk to the beneficiaries in both formal and informal sessions. It is in the informal sessions that you will learn what is really going on from their point of view. These may just be the usual complaining sessions and not to be taken seriously, but they may also reveal real problems and ways of improving the service. Do turn up unexpectedly from time to time, which is when you may gain real insight into what is actually happening locally, but beware of alienating workers by seeming to be trying merely to catch them out.

Praising staff when things go well and helping them when they go wrong are two of the keys to good management.

The first step is to set the task, and when it should be done, then to check on progress and finally to evaluate. If staff feel a valued part of the team with regular contact and the ability to talk to others who do their job elsewhere, they are much less likely to become disillusioned. That social contact with many people and not just their manager playing the 'Big Brother' role means a lot. News about the rest of the organisation formally through newsletters and informally through people calling up to say, "Have you heard…?" is an essential part of the fabric of work.

In the next chapter we will move from looking at individual workers to the terrible case of zombie charities.

8   Zombie charities

You may be familiar with zombie companies, as the term surfaced in 2008 when many companies were kept alive by constant bail-outs or interest-only repayments on their loans rather than capital repayments. In the US this term was often used about companies that received funding under the Troubled Asset Relief Program (TARP), but generally came to be used about companies that only survive because they manage to attract new funds faster than their debts can pull them under. Naturally this state of affairs rarely lasts and once a company is designated a zombie in the media its chances of raising new funds and surviving plummet. The Institute for Turnaround (IFT) which deals with companies in financial difficulty has estimated that in 2013 there were 100,000 zombie companies in the UK alone.

Zombie charities are in the same sinking boat and are perhaps more vulnerable as they are often run by charismatic individuals who, whilst they do not have a sound understanding of finance, can charm money from donors for a while because they plead a very strong emotional case. In the early years this may be no bad thing. However, once staff and beneficiaries become dependent on this uncertain flow of money, the organisation needs to build its reserves and only take on the work it can truly manage. Many smart funders will not give the kind of grant that would unbalance an organisation's income or make it dependent on receiving the same grant year after year. This may limit the charity's speed of growth and may mean that not as many people are helped as quickly as envisaged, but in the long term it is likely to result in a more stable organisation that meets many more needs.

When a charity meets a funder's objectives exactly (be that a grant-making trust, individual or government), it is easy to give to a charming and caring director who patently doesn't understand finance, but who will be terribly reassuring about the stability of the organisation. At least until next year when it needs a somewhat *larger* grant to see it out of its present difficulties all the while helping *many* more people.

This seems to have been the case with Kids Company where the director was a nationally known character with an excellent track record of working with the most difficult children eloquently describing their needs and what Kids Company did for them. Though she claimed that the finances were in order as the organisation had passed its audit each year, it could nevertheless not survive without ever-larger doses of funds. That was the effect of spending all its money each year and not building up the reserves that would have given it a cushion when income dropped. Towards the end, and after a £3m government grant, the charity survived for only a handful of weeks with much of said grant reportedly going to pay staff wages.

The auditors had cited the need for reserves in the accounts lodged at the Charity Commission and the finance directors drew the board's attention to this on more than one occasion. Not surprisingly, Kids Company lost two senior finance officers in three years prior to its closure. The board signed off the accounts. Presumably trustees did read them before signing off on them. Kids Company does not appear to have been entirely dependent on grants from government and had a fairly well-balanced set of income streams from wealthy individuals, grants and the public as well as the government, so it seems unlikely that a lack of diverse funds was at the root of their problems.

Charities, however, are in a particularly disadvantageous position when it comes to building up a reserve. Grants from institutions, whether trust, foundation, government or company, tend to be for very specific purposes on which the reporting of money spent is rightly strict. They may give, say, 10% towards overheads but this is rarely enough to cover the central costs of administering the project. That leaves money from trading, individuals and selling services to fund reserves and all of them can be problematic.

Trading is not a charitable activity and so charities cannot undertake more than a very small amount of buying and selling without setting up a separate company which then deeds some of its profit back to the charity, after allowing for tax, investment and its own reserves. Some charities like Oxfam run second-hand clothing shops or bookshops, which may also buy goods for resale. These operations are run from a separate commercial entity which, incidentally, allows the charity not to mention the trading company's overheads when they include its income in their accounts.

Selling goods or services, however, may be part of the charity's 'primary purpose' as defined in its Mems & Arts, for example, a charitable theatre company selling tickets or a care home charging its residents. In these cases the charity may not need to set up a separate company, but legal advice should always be taken. In either case these income streams can be used more easily than grants to help build reserves, as they are not as strictly earmarked for other purposes. Building reserves is part of the trustees' duty to establish sound finances for their charity.

Funds from wealthy individuals or the public can also be used for the purpose of building reserves provided it is not stated that all the funds from the appeal made to them will go in their entirety to other purposes. Of course, explaining to wealthy philanthropists that any significant amount of their funds will go into reserves is not the most attractive of pitches.

Maybe it was this reluctance that helped fuel Kids Company's failure to build reserves, or perhaps it was the director's desire to turn no child away. Whatever it was, the exponential growth countrywide with an eye on the overseas market meant that it grew like a Ponzi scheme. If an entity balloons rapidly it will burst if it cannot pay its wages and other due calls on its income.

The time to worry

The time to worry is on day one when someone thinks of setting up a charity and is full of plans about the good it will do in the world, but is less clear about how the work will be undertaken professionally and how it will be financed. Like any business, a charity needs a business plan and part and parcel of that is a sustainable fundraising strategy. If there is no time or inclination to take professional advice, or plan and discuss how the organisation will be managed and financed, then perhaps it should not be set up at all. Perhaps the potential founder's energy would be better spent helping an existing charity in the same field. Just because you feel it is important to help solve a problem does not mean that any institution or person is obliged to support you. Some of the most indignant people I have met are those whose funding request has just been turned down. Yet reviewing their application, they have made no attempt to help the donor as they have presented a demand for funds with little proof that they can carry out the work required. Just because someone has noticed an acute need doesn't mean they are the right person to set up an organisation to meet that need.

A serious case for support will demonstrate that the problem actually exists, and give quantified and qualified information on the subject, providing research references to facilitate checking by a potential funder. The case for support will then show what the organisation intends to do about the problem, namely how it will do its work and what effect that will have on the problem. It will also demonstrate its competence and track record in undertaking such work. Finally the case for support will set out how its work will be monitored and evaluated and this depends on how it measures the steps it has taken to reduce the problem. If a charity cannot measure the results of its work then it should go back to the drawing board and it is probably intending to carry out work that will be ineffective. This process means setting up a logical framework (commonly called a log-frame) for the organisation. It sets out the need in detail, inputs required of the organisation's staff, outputs (or what results from the inputs) and how the work is to be measured. A full-blown case for support will also have case studies to show changes in the lives of individuals for whom the organisation works, as well as a list of influential supporters to demonstrate that others outside the organisation recognise its good work. The case for support may also include qualifications of key staff to show that they have the necessary experience to do the work as well as lots more detailed information about the work itself.

The business plan is different again and I won't go into the details of how that is set out, as there are a lot of useful examples on the Internet. Simply put it will show over the next few years the work that will be done, the people who will be needed to do the work, any equipment etc. and how it will all be funded. It will show the estimated income and expenditure over the next few years but more importantly it will show why the organisation thinks that money will be needed (quotations and professional opinions matter) and where the money will come from. The latter will be based on your fundraising strategy, which will show who will raise the funds, where they will come from, a schedule for that work and the balance between earmarked and unearmarked income (the latter being the building blocks for reserves). Most important of all, the investment in income-generation will be key to a sustainable fundraising programme. It seems to come as some surprise to people starting out in the charitable world that fundraising is a profession and doesn't work if handled on an amateur basis. Professionally experienced fundraising staff are required, backed by the right equipment and funds to invest in a broad range of fundraising initiatives. In the early years fundraising is all about testing and rolling out income-generating initiatives. It also comes as a shock that grant-making institutions are loath to give money to help organisations fundraise. They sometimes give to institution-building such as the development of administrative structures, processes and norms including the training of key players such as the CEO, but will not give money to hire a fundraiser or invest in fundraising. At the same time the institutions will push charities to raise more money rather than come back to them for additional grants, which of course they will be tempted to do if their fundraising is undercapitalised. A change of mind by grant-makers would massively increase charities' revenues but this remains a huge and damaging blind spot for foundations and other grant-makers.

There are a limited number of sources of income and each of these should feature in the plan unless there is a very good reason not to do so. Sometimes an organisation will receive an early government grant, linked to the number of people it works with, and the immediate temptation is to go back the next year and ask for more money to help more people. Be warned that this can be at the expense of regular fundraising. Once government funds have grown to be a very large part of an organisation's income it is hard to get proper attention or investment in conventional fundraising. That is until the day that government interests change and the grants dry up then the fundraising department may be expected to suddenly fill the gap without sufficient time or adequate investment.

On the other hand, an organisation which may be slower in growing but invests in new income streams, and does so professionally and patiently as it grows, can withstand the loss of a large grant without closing its doors. The cutting of large grants is not a rare exception, indeed it is almost the rule, as no funder wants organisations to be dependent and funders' preferences usually change over time as they move from working on one problem to another. Funders like to be innovative and look for new ways to tackle problems and they also like to deal with new problems as they arise.

All this means that for those starting organisations their initial plans must consider how they will build up their fundraising programme *and* their reserves. Starting a charity to meet a need, simply because there is currently a call for proposals to address that need, is rarely a safe endeavour. The long-term future of any organisation is addressed in its business planning which should include its business plan and its fundraising plan.

Building reserves

So how does an organisation build its reserves and avoid the need to keep borrowing funds or receiving ever-larger grants? On one hand, this is a counsel of restraint to not grow too fast and furiously. On the other hand it is a call for taking fundraising seriously as a profession rather than merely an exercise of indignant demand.

Sometimes chance plays a part; many organisations either start with a legacy or receive one quite early on and that goes straight into the piggy bank labelled 'Do not touch unless in an emergency'. Sometimes trustees or finance officers diligently tuck all legacies away into reserves. Strangely, the reserves sometimes grow so large that trusts don't see any need to give a grant as the charity has plenty of its own money to spend, but such cases are the exception. Early on in business planning it is prudent to ensure that there is a regular legacy fundraising programme in place as legacies can bring in very large sums as the support base grows. If you don't ask, you don't get, is the first rule of fundraising.

As we have seen, grants are usually targeted and ring-fenced with reporting conditions, so they can be excluded from the reserve-generation plan. Of course it should be made clear that all applications have 10% added to cover overheads. A more profitable source is the mass of donations from individual supporters, members or donors. Naturally their gifts cannot all be shuffled straight into reserves, but as the organisation plans the spending of that money on its objectives, it should take into account its need for reserves or it may be unable to meet the wishes of its supporters and fail. Traditionally, those individual supporters were built up from direct mail, inserts in magazines, door-to-door and street fundraising with some occasional print advertising. Now various social media paths have been added to these routes and, as we have seen with the 2015 surge in Labour Party support, social media can be used to raise hundreds of thousands of supporters at the right time for the right cause.

Large and significant donations from wealthy individuals are sometimes in a hybrid between trust grants and supporters' gifts. Many high-net-worth individuals (HNWIs) will give through their own charitable trust and this gift may or may not come with strings attached. If it does, those strings are no less important than those of a formal foundation with multiple staff and rigid rules. If it is a more personal gift then by all means a proportion of that gift can probably be used to help build up reserves.

Money from events such as auctions, sponsored walks or concerts can also be used, providing no guarantee has been given about how the money will be used. This is a balance that must be struck and it lies between promising that all the money will be used for a very specific purpose and that the money will be used to help the charity meet its aims and objectives in more general terms. The former, of course, being a stronger ask.

Another thing that seems to have gone wrong at Kids Company is that the internal checks and balances didn't work. The auditors raised their concerns and the financial professionals passed these on to the trustees, and presumably to the chair and honorary treasurer, who would in any case sign off the accounts. The latest accounts lodged with the Charity Commission show that in the Annual Report & Accounts 2013, Kids Company (officially Keeping Kids Company) saw that:

"The greatest risk within Kids Company is deemed to be the risk of Kids Company not taking action where action is required in order to safeguard the vulnerable young people we work with, and maintain their best interests."

The second greatest risk was the reserves, but in the next column detailing the management of that risk it stated:

"Our business model is to spend money according to need, which is consistently growing. We aspire to build up our reserves when circumstances allow. Kids Company has a dedicated fundraising team."

The first sentence here shows that when faced with the bottomless pit that is sadly the needs of vulnerable children, the business model was 'spend, spend, spend'. This is no business model at all but a recipe for disaster. Having said that, it is only fair to point out that charities are perhaps not the most professional when it comes to the scrutiny of the accounts at trustee level, due to the part-time voluntary nature of the trustees and their lack of experience. This has been a constant theme in the discussions about charity management for many years.

Then again even the financial world has not acquitted itself with any particular glory in its own business practices in recent years.

It appears that the best way to avoid becoming a zombie charity is to take no comfort in the mere passing of accounts or have faith that the trustees know what they are doing. What is needed is that individuals at all levels, especially senior management, be alert to the problems that can occur and to face up to any attempt to brush financial worries under the nearest carpet. This may involve standing up to passionate and forceful leaders but it has to be done. Such scrutiny is most likely to occur in organisations where asking challenging questions is in its DNA and financial prudence is respected and not left out of the company's business model.

I have known some brilliant honorary treasurers who were very clear that they would not pass budgets that were not realistic and would not countenance spending that endangered the organisation. Invariably they had a strong financial background in commercial firms and the best of them were still at work and dealing with significant sums. Retirement and a non-financial background tended to mean they were willing to sign anything and could be persuaded to agree to things that they found challenging. Most appalling of all was that what challenged them was merely the usual investment required to generate a heathy income for the organisation. At the very least an understanding of income-generation in charities should be a requirement for becoming a treasurer; or at least the ability to acquire such knowledge with alacrity followed by an understanding of the fundraising strategy.

Bringing down the house

Zombie charities are not too dissimilar to zombie companies; they both exhibit the same tendency to live beyond their means and both have, perhaps surprisingly, a fundamental advantage over their competitors. Namely, they are not repaying capital or building reserves so they have more money to spend on development. They are often growing fairly rapidly which helps them to borrow more money or receive grants because of their apparent ability to repay the loan, meet acute needs or stabilise their finances at some future date.

When large sums have been invested in an organisation there is a huge reluctance to pull the plug and see that investment go down the drain as the organisation sinks. This is especially true when the organisation is a charity and the people it helps are vulnerable or in need. This is doubly true when the beneficiaries are kids that no one else seems able to reach. In such cases bad behaviour becomes an asset, albeit of a dubious and usually limited nature. As we have seen with Ponzi schemes, however, people's belief in magic is insatiable and continues way past any serious reality check especially when they have invested very large sums.

The way out of this situation is to cut back promptly on unsustainable growth and do not set out to cure the whole world at breakneck speed. Take a measured approach to organisational development and as the organisation grows take on experts and listen to them. Nothing is more disheartening for professional staff than their advice being ignored at the peril of the charity. One canary in this particular mine is the turnover of top financial staff, whether at board or senior manager level (or even voluntary financial advisors at the outset). This may be accompanied by complaints that grants, or other gifts, have not been used properly as the organisation struggles to meet urgent financial needs not related to the areas for which it finds it easy to raise funds.

One of my clients in the north of England, previously unknown to me, had just that problem, which manifested itself in not paying certain bills, including mine. Asking around I discovered that some commercial suppliers were becoming used to converting services that should be paid for into gifts when payment was not forthcoming. Unfortunately I was in no such position and I was eventually paid after a long haul through traditional debt recovery procedures. It was not long after that the charity brought a venture philanthropist in to fund the organisation. He made a large grant but cannily he also nominated one of his people to sit on the board. As the nominee went through the accounts and questioned people he found the true financial situation had been carefully concealed, and thousands of pounds was owed to numerous people. This had been hidden by the organisation's ability to raise fresh grants to pay off past debts. The nub of this problem lay in a simple management failure to lay off staff when the money was not there to pay them. Over a surprisingly short time the problem had become acute and the philanthropist's money was the last in a long line of increasingly large gifts that were unable to improve the situation. Under his insistence a painful cutting back of services and staff led to the organisation getting back on its financial feet and beginning to grow again... but on a sound basis this time.

The lesson here is that a charity's finances are prone to rise and fall as they are often influenced by large periodic grants or by legacies which, by their nature, cannot be easily planned. Legacies are not earmarked and therefore represent a windfall unless the budget process has included them at an unrealistically high level. The real problem is what to do when, say, a three-year grant for a staff post comes to an end. The smart CEO warns the employee from the start and is prepared to let them go, and their work to cease if no other source of income is forthcoming, hard as that might be. The much less smart director will say, "Don't worry we will find the money somehow," which is when robbing Peter to pay Paul can become institutionalised.

In the last recession, zombie banks have been in the news and the media has coined the phrase 'too big to fail' about them as well as other companies whose failure would have such repercussions for others that government cannot allow them to go under. In this case government has to take them over and inject funds or recapitalise them without nationalisation. It would be a foolish charity that thought it was too big to fail, or that its work was so important that it could not go under, however much investment had gone into its growth.

Some years back a major funder in the education field had two units, one of which vetted applications and the other of which approved them; unfortunately neither appeared to pay attention to the budget, and schools across the country ended up with half-built buildings and promises of funds suddenly withdrawn. Government refused to honour these commitments and the funder was replaced with another that exhibited rather more financial acumen. Unfortunately, funds from government for further education have been cut back considerably and further education (FE) colleges are now taking on development departments to help them raise funds along the lines of the American educational model. With professional help there is no reason why this should not be successful though many still prefer the option of government funding. We may now see zombie organisations emerge in the FE sector, as they seem to be doing in the health and other sectors. In these cases this is not so much a case of mismanagement as a shift of funding streams and a considerable drop in total funding.

Once again, the response has to be cutting back on the services if money is not forthcoming to fund the sector. This will no doubt continue the shrinking of the state, but will avoid the larger more dramatic collapse that occurs when an organisation staggers on in the belief that funds will eventually come from somewhere.

Five thoughts:

1. It would be useful for the Charity Commission to keep records of charity accounts digitally so that we could look at the metadata and draw useful conclusions about the sector. Is it really stuffed full of over-extended zombies? What kind of growth or shrinkage are we seeing in charity income? What sort of asset base do charities have in general? Is it sufficient? There is an almost endless list of questions that would help us to understand the sector and to take corrective action to keep it financially healthy. A warning could be given when accounts move out of kilter with good practice; which of course may

happen from time to time, but it is obvious that many founders and directors think getting through the audit means their finances are all in order.

2. Government could develop an investment fund aimed at funding professional fundraising for those charities they witness taking over some of the burdens of the welfare state, or which could be used to invest with easy repayment terms by any charity that could demonstrate it had valid plans in place. This may follow the pattern of venture philanthropists who invest in charities but expect a return, and the Grameen Bank's programme of making small loans to individuals, often called 'microfinance'.

3. Charities are sometimes sitting on huge assets in the shape of their inner-city HQs and other buildings, which were bought some time ago and are now extremely valuable compared to the turnover of the organisation, which may have shrunk. Like any asset, the value of these buildings can be realised if the organisation is in trouble, but in a couple of cases which I know, the buildings went down with the charity when it was closed or merged with another charity. Trustees looking ahead could have averted these crises if they had been willing to agree on disposing of the asset to help the beneficiaries.

4. Trustees can be a nightmare all of their own, with no proper terms of service, no understanding of finance,

fundraising or the legal issues of running a charity and it may be time for more stringency and less hand-wringing, at least to ensure the efficacy of the largest charities. The organisation that should probably be responsible is the Charity Commission but it has long ceased to be any kind of effective watchdog, if it ever was, and successive governments have failed to build any other kind of institution. The result? The whole sector of charities, trusts and foundations remains idiosyncratic and relatively ungoverned in any consistent or effective manner.

5. We should all be aware of our legal responsibilities and though we may know all about the work of the organisation, be able to speak passionately about the people we help or the environment, once we are in positions of authority it is beholden on us to understand finance and fundraising. It is not enough just to listen and take advice from the professionals. A real understanding is required so that we can ask critical questions and comprehend the accounts for ourselves. A series of short courses may save your career and the charity you care so much about.

A case study – Japan feeds its zombies

Probably the longest running and most widespread zombie businesses are in Japan, and there are grounds for thinking much of the economy has been zombified since around 1997, with thousands of zombie companies whose existence the government has recently admitted. These companies are kept afloat by loans from banks which could themselves be classed as zombies as they in turn are fed by government to keep them alive. As consumption and production fell, the government increased consumption taxes to balance its books, which further held back demand.

Japan has tried many things to solve this problem apart from letting the businesses go under. The latter is an obvious solution but it would prompt real pain before the assets of these businesses could be productively recycled into growth thus stimulating the taxes which currently elude the government. Of course, zombie companies pay no tax as they don't make a profit. Growth in Japan has been static for as long as many people can remember though it is still the world's third largest economy by gross domestic product (GDP) after the US and China, but ahead of Germany et al. And so strangely the experience of a major economy resonates with some UK charities.

Japan is also haunted by the spectre of deflation which prevents people buying goods they feel may be cheaper in future and prevents investment as the returns on goods are close to zero.

Japan's Prime Minister, Shinzo Abe, has tried a three-pronged attack, which involves monetary easing, fiscal stimulus and structural reforms (often called 'Abenomics') to kick-start the dormant economy, but it has proved highly resistant. The lower yen resulting from quantitative easing has meant exports have had a better time, but imports which most Japanese rely on have been more expensive, threatening consumption, and tax rises have also cut consumption, though unemployment has fallen and wages are rising slightly.

What does this mean for charities – if anything? There is a fear that many UK charities are really zombies (due to the money they have borrowed and cannot pay back) and any serious rise in interest rates will knock them out as their borrowings will become unsustainable, but Japan's example shows that it is not that easy to recover from a recession using the tools that governments now favour. Low interest rates at least give charities a breathing space to first recognise the problem, then check if they have it and finally to take corrective action by building funds that can be used to reduce debt ahead of any recovery and accompanying interest rate rises.

This situation may require a distinct alteration in income streams to replace borrowed money with funds that have been gifted to them, for example boosting membership or major donor income from HNWIs. Headquarter buildings could be sold and larger-than-expected cuts in services taken, so that the organisation will be put on a financially sound footing. Each organisation will have its own remedies depending on its level of debt or other problems, and these remedies will almost invariably circle around cutting services and investing in a professional fundraising programme aimed at sustainable growth.

9 Are vampires worse than zombies?

Sometimes charities have a director who is the figurehead and a deputy director who runs the day-to-day work of the charity. When they complement each other this can be hugely beneficial. The director talks to the media, attracts support and enthuses the staff. The deputy director meanwhile is carrying out the people management and other operational business that the director (possibly the charismatic founder) is happy to avoid because managing people or finance is not really their thing.

One large charity I knew had grown rapidly over the years but still had its charismatic director working every day in the field and being the face of the organisation. It also had a deeply insecure deputy who had been a trustee previously and appeared one day as the deputy director, at a significant salary, in the days before the senior management team was in place. The deputy maintained a direct line to the chair of the board as well as the other trustees, whom she knew well. She made sure he was covered at every turn.

Unfortunately, the new deputy was no more capable of professional management than the founder and preferred to run things behind the scenes with favourites and enemies and a tendency to fix meetings, consultations and interviews beforehand. The organisation was well funded but staff morale and performance were at rock bottom.

Appointing favourites with little regard to competence and undermining those who presented any kind of challenge meant that the beneficiaries often had less-than-optimum help. The very structures that should have delivered the best service to the right people were staffed by people who didn't know how to make sound decisions. Worse still any great ideas that other people had were welcomed then ignored or marginalised. As a result, staff turnover was high. Staff had breakdowns. The best people were paid off quietly when they were deemed to pose a threat.

One member of staff, who tended to be interviewed by the media instead of the director who regularly refused to comment to the media, was told to stop. He was hurt and rather baffled as part of his job was to represent the organisation but he was offered a tidy sum to leave, which he did. He had the foresight to know that had he stayed he would have been hounded out eventually. Another staff member was encouraged to approach a wealthy relative for money. When the relative refused to donate the staff member was criticised for being 'unhelpful' and told to keep trying. Other staff who were felt to be getting too big for their boots, merely because their efforts were appreciated by grateful beneficiaries, were reduced to part-time work or asked to move to another department.

It seems extraordinary now that nothing was done. The director thought that his deputy was his friend and confidante; the deputy felt she had the chair of the board and a few other cronies in tow and it seemed nothing could be done. It was only when a group of staff got together, documented what was happening and demanded that the board take action did it seem that things might change. But it was too late by then as people were beginning to distrust each other, there was no union representation and a seemingly acquiescent board felt there was nothing they could do, leaving staff to suffer in silence.

After a few years it became obvious that the deputy was after the director's job and was putting it about that he was unfit to continue and that it was time he retired. Things seemed to be happening behind the scenes and doors were heard banging. The director did indeed retire. Much to everyone's surprise a search committee of the deputy's favourites failed to register the heavy hints that came their way and picked an outsider and much to everyone's relief the deputy gave up in a huff, disgusted at not being chosen after all her scheming.

It took many years for the organisation to right itself internally. Poor appointments had been made because staff were favourites or had worked for the director's favourite charity and were automatically deemed to be excellent, undermined the quality of work. Most importantly the processes didn't work in the interests of the beneficiaries but in the interests of making life easy for the staff. As for the managers, who should have sorted the mess, they were unimaginative and fearful of starting any new initiatives or improvements. In time, the new director got to grips with the organisation making new appointments at senior manager level and empowering them to carry out constructive change below. The board, once stripped of its power to interfere directly in staff matters and without its behind-the-scenes briefings, also began to change and the old guard slowly moved on, allowing the organisation to renew itself.

This toxic behaviour is little short of bullying and sucks the lifeblood from an organisation. It is harder in practice to deal with than the behaviour of zombies who are passively useless. Toxic behaviour may stem from a lack of ability to do the job properly and the vampire, instead of accepting this and undertaking training for the right skills, reverts to playground tactics and devious traits which they feel have helped them in the past. Sometimes vampires may just feel that this is the way to manage, and have a somewhat paranoid view of the word whereby transparent management decisions are thought to invite criticism that they don't feel capable of handling.

So back to the question at the head of this chapter: yes, vampires can be worse than zombies. Maybe we should be grateful that zombies most probably outweigh vampires in the workforce – what a thought!

Vampires are toxic people

Usually vampires are not in high-profile leadership positions and can therefore be tackled more easily. We probably all know toxic individuals who disrupt their colleagues and departments, upset people and cause tension and animosity, all of which is debilitating for everyone who comes into contact with them. This can be serious and cause psychological distress to individuals. It saps time and energy just to survive in the bad atmosphere that these people create. It has a stultifying effect on the work and prevents people enjoying their lives.

Sometimes this behaviour is caused by insecurity which results in an overwhelming desire for controlling although this is never stated explicitly. The toxic individual prefers to undermine people and, as we saw above, will promote favourites or people who will present no challenge. These toxic types hate other people voicing their ideas for fear it will highlight their incompetence. The result is that they prevent the innovators from carrying out new work in order to prevent being shown up for their own lack of new ideas. Sometimes they micromanage as a means of ensuring that others do not shine. Their lack of confidence means that some become the office know-it-all, even though they do not know it all, rather than get left behind in the new ideas department.

Arrogance is also a sign of a toxic individual. Arrogant people despise others and won't let anyone challenge their feeling of superiority. On the other hand self-confidence is a positive quality and self-confident people are not afraid of other people's opinions or success. Arrogance crushes staff, leading to immense frustration, and it often means that the best solutions do not always prevail. Having to implement someone else's sub-par idea is no fun at all.

Toxic people often lie and at first this is hard to detect. We all work on a 'trust first' basis. When a colleague says something, we believe it, as we have no reason to doubt them. But toxic individuals lie to their colleagues and worse still they lie *about* their colleagues, which is where they become really dangerous, as people begin to doubt each other and harbour unfounded suspicions. You cannot trust toxic people and if they work with you they poison working relationships, which makes it impossible to do the work properly. Always promising and never delivering can be highly debilitating in a subordinate, but in a boss it can be very disquieting.

Many toxic people jump to conclusions about others and criticise them relentlessly. This is about attacking people and lacks the objectivity of a reasoned judgement; it means forming opinions quickly and is often rooted in personal prejudice. Incorrect assumptions are made and then acted upon.

The flip side of the coin from arrogance is the person who is always complaining they are being treated unfairly, their boss hates them, their mother and father never loved them, their colleagues despise them and nothing is ever their fault. Do not mistake this for humility as they are choosing to be a victim and describing the world in terms of its negative effect on them. Their glass is not half empty, someone else has already drunk half of their glass and is probably coming back in a minute for the rest. These people will never be in control of their own lives, nor will they experience the joy of making a decision, acting on it and then, regardless of whether they succeed or fail, accepting full responsibility for their actions.

Envy is a terrible thing. The toxic individual is plagued by envy and wants any success or opportunity to be theirs and hates it if other people are honoured and they are not. Again they feel aggrieved and believe they deserve things others have or even that they should have them instead! At work this may be a promotion or an increase in salary and the toxic person may make quite ridiculous claims to either with little basis in reality. The toxicity of envious people manifests itself in claims of unfairness, which may then be championed by others causing unnecessary unpleasantness for those who have done well.

Hand in hand with envy comes greed, where people want more and more and sometimes even things that rightly belong to others. Greed can be about physical possessions, but it can also be about relationships and personal qualities like self-confidence or the ability to communicate effectively. Greed spurs a desire for more and more and can strike people at any level of society, even if the person is already very rich and very successful. When multimillionaires are asked how much they would need to feel content they often reply twice what they have now, at whatever level of income they happen to have at that time. Greed at work fuels unreasonable behaviour and if either envy or greed is given its head then it may spark off resentments that take years to calm down.

Whingeing and being negative can be an outlet for frustration but when it becomes habitual and constant it has the power to adversely affect everyone and reduce the quality of the organisation's work. It is also debilitating to disagree with whingers and face a wall of unpleasant opinions, which are often about an organisation for which you care deeply.

Spotting a toxic individual is easy if several of these behavioural traits are displayed. But if someone has just one of them it can be harder to pin down because it seems like human nature, and we may instinctively take the easy route of agreeing but trying to stay out of their way. Actually dealing with the problem is harder but far from impossible.

What you can do about toxic people

Toxic people cause stress of the worse kind and they are dangerous to you, and to your staff, if you are a manager. You will need coping strategies until you are ready for a confrontation. You also must decide if the individual can be brought round, because they have a genuine and limited problem that can be resolved. Alternatively you may conclude that they need to leave the organisation. If the latter is the case then you need to follow the law carefully but quickly and never seek shortcuts as you are dealing with irrational behaviour. The person is unlikely to keep to agreements and may well be thinking about challenging everything you decide.

Here are my top tips for getting the most effective outcome:

1. Set your own limits on your contact with the toxic person. Decide where you can cut them out altogether. Set time limits and don't listen to everything they say uninterrupted, but above all don't wallow with them or join in their conspiracies, complaints or

victim behaviour. Don't share confidences with them as it will not be appreciated and they are likely to be repeated with a negative spin. Just deal with the facts as presented. Try not to be judgemental and have compassion for them. Their toxicity is a sign that things are not well with them. Try to cultivate understanding, respect and forgiveness so that you are not emotionally damaged by the stress they cause.

2. Pick your moment. Wait until you can change the situation, perhaps by dismissing them, and don't get involved in arguments you can't win because these are not rational people. The key is to manage your emotions and not to rise to provocation until you are ready. Don't automatically engage your emotions and react, but try to model positive behaviour, especially for subordinates and colleagues.

   Think through any strategy to dismiss them and clear it with the people above you so you have their backing. Make sure the grounds for dismissal are clear and legal. You may have to set targets for achievement and behaviour, but don't back down if this takes time and is a fraught process. You may find that you can pull the person out of their bad behaviour.

3. You are entitled to a happy, successful life. Celebrate your successes regardless of their carping and be joyful. When things go well enjoy them with your

friends, and remember you don't have to engage with people who are negative or undermining. Make sure you look after yourself until the situation is resolved, and let other people know what you are intending to do about it.

4. Leave this person behind but don't forget them. If they reappear you should ensure that you are not going back into the same old situation with them. Move on and avoid more trauma. People often just don't realise the stress they cause and will continue their behaviour until stopped or until it is overcome in some way. That is not your job if you are not a therapist.

5. Build a strong support system. There is nothing like the support of your partner, your colleagues and your boss, or if the problem is your boss, your boss's manager. Ask for their help, opinions and advice so you are not alone and ensure that you have their backing when you are about to tackle the situation. You may find there is much more support than you expect, and that can transform the situation from your personal problem to the organisation's problem, which it is.

6. All the emotional intelligence gurus say that you must get some sleep to lower your stress level and to recharge your batteries. This may be hard if the stress is what keeps you awake at night. Try to move your

mind away from the problem to something more restful each time you find yourself obsessing. Look at the positive things in your life, which will help you to be more creative in finding a solution to the problem. A positive outlook appears to engender creativity.

7. Focus on solutions and a successful outcome to the problems created by the toxic person. Think about how will you handle them rather than how painful they are.

8. As well as a physical boundary also maintain an emotional distance. Think about your own emotions and safeguard them by smiling, nodding and moving on. Remain calm under pressure. Check any inclination you may have for negative self-talk and be compassionate about yourself. You are not that person, you are separate, different and you can deal with the situation.

Conclusions

Most toxic individuals are not open to reason so establish the facts and deal only with those. This is particularly important if you are going to dismiss them, but their effect on other people is a fact too and one you may need to document. Make sure you talk to a wide variety of people affected by the individual and keep a record of what they say. This documenting process can in itself can be a revelation to you and probably to the toxic person.

You cannot afford to let a bully terrorise your staff and the actions of these people in causing stress amounts to bullying. This gives you a clear mandate to deal with the problem, but remember that you are probably dealing with a damaged and irrational person, not someone who is merely an occasional schemer. They will not suddenly behave rationally so be on your guard against outbursts or other bad behaviour, as they are sure to happen.

Toxic people may be charming when it suits them. Do not let yourself be taken in but look at how they treat other people. They are usually selfish and cannot see the point in helping people who cannot help them. They also lie and this habit can make them hard to discipline. Be clear, insistent and enforce what you say as this will help you get around their evasiveness. They may try to succeed by underhand means as they hate not getting their own way and when it comes to this state of affairs dismissal may be on the cards.

Stress good and bad...

In the workplace we can come under all kinds of stress, some of which is quite acceptable and can propel us to achieve great things. This kind of stress is natural and can be a source of creativity and innovation as we try to do better than our competitors or strive to develop our organisation and help more people. This is good stress and not a problem. On occasion it may keep us up all night due to a creative high rather than despondent thoughts.

The kind of stress that toxic individuals cause is harmful and if it goes on long enough it can cause us physiological and psychological changes. This kind of stress must be stopped quickly. And sometimes this means a move sideways or leaving to join a new organisation. Should you opt to leave always ensure that decision-makers know why you are leaving and give them a clear, written record of what has occurred. These may be the same people who did not help when asked and they may have had good reason for not helping, but you still need to ensure your point of view is on the record.

There are many coping strategies to deal with stress. These are useful but the real cause of the stress needs to be confronted and changed by those who are in a position to do so. This may be the CEO or the chair of the board. When these people act like zombies and don't carry out their duty the organisation loses its best people quickly – why should they stay around to be affected by the toxic person, either directly or indirectly? I have seen belligerent staff revolts due to trivial matters because a toxic individual had turned the staff against a manager. It is where the constant undermining, complaining and fibbing begins to wreak havoc, which is why early action to quell such behaviour is essential to prevent bad behaviour spreading.

One source of stress is an unduly heavy workload with which we simply cannot cope. Often it is in our nature to do our best to deal with the impossible rather than to recognise it for what it is and refuse to accept the workload or to leave the job. We may have undeserved feelings of failure because we could not achieve the impossible. Whilst unpleasant it is a lesser evil than the extreme effects of stress where people die as a result. Those who commission such a workload must be confronted and they have to deal with the situation that caused the problem in the first instance. Poor managers who don't recruit in time to fill empty posts, or toxic individuals who deliberately overburden staff so that they will fail, need to be challenged from below and from above.

Social engagement, talking to people face to face, receiving positive feedback and sympathetic listening can calm the usual stress responses of 'flight or fight'. This occurs when we have so much threatening stress that our metabolism speeds up and our bodies are flooded with adrenaline and cortisol which prepares us to fight or to run away from danger, i.e. the stress. Similarly social interaction helps when we reach the other stress point of freezing and being unable to move. This was useful for our distant ancestors when not moving made them less visible to predators and fainting allowed them to play dead for a while. Today those reflexes are not always useful. Stress-induced rigidity and the inability to make a decision about what to do next, or which problem to solve first, can be devastating to a usually productive and hard-working person.

This is why your support network is so important. It can be your friends, family and work colleagues, but however it is composed it will help you when you are stressed. If you have no support system you may be much more vulnerable to stress. Time spent building and maintaining friendships with colleagues is invariably worthwhile when you are threatened by vampires. Friends will help keep you sane and prevent you too turning into one of those whingeing vampires.

Your network also helps with confidence and a confident person will more easily combat stress as they feel they are in charge of their lives and that the current situation will be overcome in time. If you feel everything is out of your control, stress is much harder to deal with and indeed may overpower you. A positive attitude and optimistic outlook can keep stress at bay as it helps you feel that change *will* come and will be a good thing when it does.

It always helps to have a sense of humour, which can stop you falling into despair, as you can see the funny side of even the most trying circumstances. Humour can also help you to control your emotions and to calm you down so you can bounce back from life's hard knocks. Laughter is one of life's great healers and joking with your mates is a great way to dispel the gloom that pervades the workplace when a vampire is doing their worst.

After reading this you will now be more prepared for an encounter with a vampire. Knowledge and readiness go hand in hand as a bulwark against the toxic individuals that may stalk your life.

Reflections

In many ways this is the most important chapter of this book as it tackles the times when difficulties seem overwhelming and threaten to destroy you mentally and physically. This is no exaggeration as bad stress over prolonged periods is known to affect both the mind and the body. Your boss may be merely a well-meaning zombie but that could be enough to infect your life with a high level of stress over time. This in turn may cause you serious problems that make you unable to cope with the easiest decisions or tasks. You have the power to make things better in order to recover even if it means moving on to another job.

Typifying people as vampires and zombies may seem a rather glib thing, designed to be on trend, but it does help to characterise problem people and think seriously about their effect in the workplace and on our lives. As a result when we do encounter these people we will be better equipped to deal with them rather than letting problems escalate. It will mean that we won't allow bad behaviour to prevail nor will we allow it to be brushed under the nearest carpet. And we won't reward bad behaviour by paying people off and moving them on to wreak havoc elsewhere.

In the blogs that preceded this book and brought it to life, real-life cases were used with a large dose of camouflage. People responded by circulating them to each other in departments struggling with just such problems. This viral rush showed that a nerve had been touched. The problem was not just in my experience or in my mind, but haunted the work of many people across all sectors, not just the third sector. The feedback the blogs attracted served to map out new areas for this book and though it is not possible to cover all interpersonal problems that occur at work, it tries to deal with the key ones that keep people up at night.

The two most influential figures in most people's lives are their partner and their boss and often they spend more time with their boss than their partner. When this relationship goes wrong, or your boss does not sort out toxic behaviour in colleagues, this can place a huge strain on other parts of your life. It is not always easy or even possible to move jobs, so coping strategies are extremely useful. For me these strategies have evolved over time and I know that they have worked in real life which is why the best are incorporated in this book.

The last word on vampires

We all feel like complaining at times but offloading is best done outside the workplace. When we complain at work it should be constructive: this is what I think is wrong, this is why I think it is wrong and this is what should be done about it, this is who should be responsible for seeing it is done and by this (realistic) date. This gives people a chance to discuss it with you and if you are wrong (always a possibility) then for you to acknowledge that. It is not constructive to go to person after person with the same story and not to listen to them. If you find yourself doing this you are probably in need of some of the advice above. If it is that important and people don't agree, or they only agree to make you go away, then it may be time to reconsider your problem or to move on.

Do you find yourself running down a colleague, or all your colleagues, to each other? Recognise what you are doing: you are trying to make yourself feel better by belittling them. Beware that this is not an effective strategy to follow – there is probably something else in your life which needs to be sorted out.

Management is about explaining to people what to do next and when to do it. You then need to ask them how they are getting on *before* the deadline, praising them if they do well or helping them to do better if they don't. It is an interactive process. Staying away and picking holes in the finished product is not an option nor is micromanaging throughout. Yes, it may be very important and you might be the best person to do the job, but it is not your job and you are paid to manage not to carry out the task. If you don't think the task will be done well then your staff may need training or guidance before they start the task, not every few minutes. Let them take responsibility and make as many decisions as possible, because that is how they will best learn.

Meetings are not something to be 'fixed' beforehand and you should not be afraid of a decision that goes against your better judgement. If it is your decision to make then take it, don't pretend there is a consultation process. If you genuinely want the opinion of others then ask them openly. Don't tell them that everyone thinks Y and that you agree it is the right thing to do. Listen to their opinion and you will certainly emerge better informed and more able to argue your case if you understand the arguments against it. Of course you might also be plain wrong!

If you are scared of chairing meetings, or of speaking at them for example in public, then look up some of the more formal rules for meetings on the Internet and take a course on speaking in public. When people have been asked to vote on something, can you take a point of order or a point of information or both? You really should know the answer to this kind of question though the situation may never arise. If you have never been trained to speak in public, maybe it is time to book a workshop or two. It is certainly one of the most useful skills to have in any job with prospects and not just for public speaking.

In the next chapters we will go beyond coping with difficult people and look at how you can transform your life, and become one of those high-achieving, charismatic individuals who transform organisations and change lives. They may appear to be born that way but the techniques that mark them out from the crowd can be learned, practised and used to enhance your life. If you are to vanquish the zombies, deal with the vampires and escape the toxicity around you, it's time to become a superhero. How? By learning from the life lessons of real superheroes and finding out how they seem to walk through life so effortlessly. Hint: it requires application and hard work but it's worth it.

10 Enter the superhero

Many of the people who have inspired me arrived in the charities where I was working at roughly my level but stood out as people who were going much further, much faster. Something about them marked them out from day one, and way before I had moved on, or moved up, they were at the next stage of their trajectory. There was always something about their self-confidence, their easy relationship with those above them and their ability to get on with people that really impressed my more introvert self. I wanted to be their friend – at least at work.

Bernie was the first person I noticed who stood out in this way. He was working at the charity before I arrived and on my first day he introduced himself and offered to show me around. By the end of the tour I knew the football team he supported (Arsenal) and that he was married with a child. He knew a little about me – I didn't support Arsenal – but we were both studying for a degree in the evenings. Later the other staff asked if I had noticed his socks, which I had as they were green and they seemed to be a topic of interest as he always wore green socks. The one day he wore black socks, he was asked who had died.

In my first staff meeting I noticed too that he spoke early and articulately about one of his projects and wasn't afraid to comment on other proposals arguing against any idea where he felt something wasn't right. He didn't feel obliged to talk about everything or about things where he did not have a view. It was immediately apparent that he was someone you would want on your side, and when he was allied with the CEO the others tended to agree. That is not to say he would never disagree with the CEO; he did, and he was prepared to argue his case in a reasonable manner. He had a view and often a comment on most things that were happening across the charity, even when he wasn't involved, and we were not surprised that he was selected for a joint management and staff discussion team. He had made it clear he was interested in the charity's wider remit, which quickly separated him from those of us who were really interested only in our own neck of the woods. Life was tough enough without engaging in things like the restructuring processes with which head office seemed obsessed.

Bernie's greatest challenge came from a junior staff member who wasn't doing his job well and showed all of the signs that he wasn't really interested. He was late for meetings and scruffy when he should have been smartly presented. Volunteers who reported to him tended to ignore him and persisted in doing things that the organisation had stopped doing some time ago, for fear of damaging its reputation. Bernie had a word and set him some tasks. They were done, but rather hurriedly and ineffectively compared to the rest of us who had, it must be noted, carried out all the tasks a long time ago. We saw them both meeting several times and the junior staff member was heard to say that he wasn't leaving and what's more he was going to report Bernie for harassment. This went on for some time and then suddenly he was gone. Bernie announced that he had sacked him, which came as a great shock. People just didn't get sacked from that charity and there were plenty more staff reporting to different managers who were much worse. We all waited for the comeback from the CEO or an industrial tribunal or just for some calamity to befall Bernie, but nothing happened. He had cleared it with the CEO and followed the correct procedure and that was that.

Bernie then made two jumps in quick succession. The first was to a position in the head office, and then barely two years later he had a significant promotion to another charity, after which I lost touch with him. Some years later I saw he was mentioned in an article and noticed that he had an MBA, so his studying had paid off. He was now the director of an international charity with a good reputation.

I tried to follow in his footsteps, but lacking what appeared to be his natural abilities I tried to acquire them by making sure that I went on as many relevant training courses as I could; I attended those offered by the charity, and some external courses which focussed on my skills gap around presentations and public speaking. Bernie was the first of my superheroes who stood out because he was not arrogant and he did not need to put people down to deal with any lack of inner security. He didn't seem to compete but knew where he was going, so he had no need to crush others to get where he wanted to be. Actually he seemed very interested in the success of his colleagues, who occasionally followed him when he moved.

Other superheroes included a CEO who managed his board very well and I followed his technique when I reached that level. At my first trustees' meeting I explained to them very carefully and clearly why they could not carry out work themselves and then charge the charity a fat fee. "Hah," I thought, "that is one lesson well learned – how to deal with trustees." Then they sacked me so I had to revise my rules of engagement. It was still an invaluable lesson I had learned, that simply adopting another's way of managing may not work, especially if it doesn't suit the circumstances or your own character.

I learned to deal with such delicate matters only after consultation with the chair and my colleagues rather than an all-out assault on a traditional practice, however wrong-headed, especially before I became known and respected. I still maintain the basic principle of having my arguments ready in case I need to persuade a board to accept a new idea. However I would now discuss the issues and questions, rather than trying to win by diktat. Persuasion is generally a more powerful tool.

Gradually, it became clear that many of my superheroes had very similar characteristics and these were not innate skills they were born with. Instead there was a collection of useful life skills they had taken the time to acquire and which duly made them stars.

Zombies and superheroes

Zombies are a good test for superheroes. They present a challenge that other staff may have avoided or ignored for a long time. A superhero however is on a journey and knows that this is just one challenge of many they will have to face. They learn from the encounter thus making the next one easier. For superheroes it is an interesting problem precisely because other people have not solved it. Superheroes know that if they are to get all their staff working effectively, they cannot ignore someone who bucks the rules or is plain indolent. So they will most probably consult their own boss, consider the problem and devise a solution ensuring at the start of the process that they are cleared to fire the person if necessary. They will then make every effort to bring the zombie on board as a productive individual, which may take a long time during which they will look for signs of progress, or alternatively signs that this just is not going to work. If it is not working they will move to dismissal and work their way steadily through the whole process even if it is long and drawn out and rather painful.

Psychologically this is hard and, as we have seen, the zombie may well object, complain, obstruct and threaten. The superhero knows it will not last and recognises that handling such situations boosts their own confidence, increases their standing in the organisation and enhances their ability to get the best out of the rest of their team, including the new person they hire to replace the zombie. All that would not be the case if they paid them off, arranged an unnecessary restructuring or tried to make life unpleasant for the zombie in the hope they would leave.

Superheroes have other lasting benefits, one of which is that they inspire others to emulate their performance and thus improve the morale of their own staff as well as others across the organisation. Naturally their own manager feels good, as hiring them was clearly the right decision.

If they deal well with a zombie, superheroes get considerable kudos for solving what was possibly a well-known but notoriously difficult problem. Some zombies are also deeply unpleasant and frighten off lesser souls who won't tackle them. Of course, on much rarer occasions they have a connection to the board, and I have known such people being reinstated by the chair of the board after a staff member dismissed them. If that happens unchallenged then the superhero has no choice but to move on, as they will have lost the ability to discipline their staff. Chances are however that with support from senior colleagues who help in confronting the chair a resolution is possible. This is where the building of bridges, connections and networks comes in. It may seem this is a waste of time, but when you need people to speak on your behalf it is too late to build your contacts.

A good director or chair will encourage superheroes and having given them direction will keep a light hand on the reins, but won't let go entirely. Once the superhero and the director (or chair of the board) are aligned in what they want the organisation to achieve, and how to get there, others will be enthused. This is not to plead for special treatment for superheroes as it risks them losing the respect of their colleagues. Superheroes should never be seen as the creature of one individual, which can happen if they become a favourite.

Favourites are not superheroes but usually people with ability that a senior member of staff favours over other more able people, because they will do as they are bid without question. A favourite's destiny is usually linked to the rise or fall of their master.

Superheroes in conjunction with senior staff demonstrate that difficult, even great, things can be achieved and hard tasks accomplished. For them, compromise is not automatic as it robs many organisations of their ability to implement change and achieve their goals. Unfortunately, mediocrity is often the default standard that supposedly keeps everyone on board but which is unsatisfactory as it means that new ideas are resisted repeatedly, sometimes for years. It is far better to have the courage of one's convictions to carry out the consultations and make the improvements rather than making endless, unwarranted concessions to staff or others out of fear.

What does it take to become a superhero?

There are at least three steps in the journey. The first is to have the knowledge that is needed to do the tasks required by the position you hold and those you intend to hold – it is too late to 'learn on the job'. This may seem obvious yet so many people content themselves with just getting by and occasionally winging meetings. That is deeply unconvincing; a superhero will read about their subject and talk to people until they really understand the task, which might even require study sessions at home paid for out of their own pocket. This ability to acquire the information necessary to conclude their work successfully, build their CV then get the next job is a prerequisite to becoming a superhero. It isn't easy and it takes self-discipline to work and study at your own expense, in your own time, but it can make a critical difference that people respect.

The second step is to become the kind of person who impresses people, whom they remember and with whom they want to work and be friends. In this context friends does not mean 'best friends forever' or even just best friends, it means close colleagues at work. A superhero does not strive to be everyone's friend in their department. They may have to discipline them and they will have to discuss things without people either agreeing with them automatically, or feeling offended when they take a position with which their colleagues disagree.

You may have noticed that superheroes are clearly identifiable and sometimes this is done through their appearance. Perhaps they always wear a certain colour, a bow tie or very traditional clothes, but always something that marks them out. This is not to say they should wear something silly, in that 'Look at me I'm a bit of a laugh' way. It may be something quite subtle but it will always be appropriate. They will usually look like they are wearing the right clothes for the next level up, as if they were only temporarily doing their current job, which may indeed be true.

They know how to work a room, which is simply the art of going round, introducing yourself and talking to everyone. Somehow people notice superheroes when they enter a room. This is, in part, theatre: the pause to identify people, the brief handshake when greeting colleagues and the short chat with the top people in the room. Sidling in and standing quietly at the back won't get you noticed.

At meetings they are on time, have read the agenda, understand the subjects and make their views known clearly but not loudly. It is so easy to let meetings drift by and only talk when it directly concerns your work, but if you want the next job up you would be advised to show you can do it long before you apply.

Key tasks like chairing meetings, managing staff, understanding finance and fundraising need to be learnt a long time before you start, perhaps from books, courses and debating societies. Volunteering for tasks that might prove to be a relevant experience is useful as is volunteering for other charities (especially for their boards). Discussion with colleagues who can do the jobs that you find daunting is also an effective way to learn.

The third step is about your vision and your drive to get there. You will need to have clear answers to the classic question, "Where will you be in three years' time and then in five years' time?" If you know what your goals are for your career, income, home, family and the like it is so much easier to be successful. All these goals have stepping stones and when you can see your way to that great job in a series of steps it is much easier than thinking you must get there in one leap.

At each stage the task is to equip yourself with the skills you need to build the right CV for the next position and to secure the next interview. This is not a matter of skipping from job to job. There will be times when you will need to show you can stay in a job for several years. A CV where you move every eighteen months, especially after the early days, probably means you just cannot do the work.

Sometimes, when you have no clear direction, it is adequate to set up a false goal, for example, a great position you may like to have, but which doesn't yet form part of your life goals so is not something you would necessarily choose right now. Perhaps it is not too far removed from where you are now and has an attractive salary. Having picked this temporary target you can now work your way in that direction until your real path is clear. In acquiring the competence to do that job, applying for the 'stepping stones' jobs on the way, and building the contacts who could help you, it may be you find that you have not wasted any time because the path to the 'false' job begins to clarify things and you gain a much firmer idea of where you want to go and how you might get there. Your path may also divert to somewhere you really want to be, based on the work and CV you have built up.

Superheroes v vampires and zombies: top tips

1. Deal with vampires first: they are much more deadly than zombies (who can be tackled later). Because vampires infect others they can seriously damage the performance of a department or even an entire organisation. They work behind the scenes to destabilise others whereas zombies are inclined to do very little and only react if prodded firmly.

Picking off vampires sends a clear signal to your staff that you will not tolerate underhand unpleasantness and that staff morale is important to you. If you tackle the zombies first, the vampires will see you coming and work against you.

2. So how do you detect vampires? It is often easier than you think. The first thing vampires try is to get you on side in one of their schemes to see if you will play ball with them. It may be bad-mouthing the person you report to, asking you to argue for a certain action that benefits them, or telling you that an enemy of theirs is telling people you are no good and spreading lies about you. The latter scenario is all too common and shows the complex nature of the vampire's world. So who do you believe? That will soon become clear as you talk to the staff and only if you are susceptible to gossip, and deeply insecure

yourself, will you go along with what they say. They are not your friend and trusting them to keep you informed about what is going on is a fatal mistake.

3. Tackling vampires is not as straightforward as tackling zombies – give me a zombie any day! The first step is to make it clear you do not operate in this manner and you don't expect them to do so. Talk to your manager and obtain their agreement that the person's actions are undermining other staff members. Document what is happening in detail and what you are doing about it. Deal with the facts not the personality, and don't get angry. List as many instances of their bad behaviour as you can find, and see what backup for this you can get from other staff. Find another manager, preferably your own, who can bear witness to what is happening and its impact.

Next, confront the vampire to stop their malign behaviour. Talk through all the instances of what they have done, the effect it has had on others and make it clear this is against the organisation's ethos. Tell the vampire to cease this behaviour and how they must act differently in future.

Find out what motivates this sort of behaviour and offer your support for change. Consider if there is a genuine grievance lurking there which can be resolved. Of course the vampire may need counselling if their behaviour is due to personal issues and this might be a positive outcome.

Follow up this meeting with regular set meetings to monitor what is happening, and to show you are not going to let this pass without change. Make sure it features in any performance reviews. Praise good behaviour and criticise any reoccurrence of bad behaviour.

If all that doesn't work you have a well-documented path towards dismissal.

4. Be clear that bullying and harassment are different, more obvious and in many ways easier to deal with, and how to do that is well documented in the literature on human resources and management so we will not go that far here.

Bullying is intimidating, threatening behaviour that is often offensive and humiliating, designed to force the person to do something or to control and subjugate them. It is malicious and may even cause injury.

Harassment is repeated unwanted conduct usually to do with sex, gender, race or sexual orientation and is often very close to bullying. A person's behaviour may be both at the same time.

Bullying and harassment are far from the very positive, strong management which may give repeated negative feedback if the person's work is poor, but is constructive and supportive, designed to help the person develop. It does not undermine their dignity, humiliate or denigrate them.

The superhero's management style

The superhero's style of management is flexible; they are not locked into any one style, which is a great advantage because each group of people and tasks may require a different style for them to be led effectively. A superhero can adapt their style to the circumstances, which may vary from organisation to organisation or team to team.

Sometimes the rather old-fashioned style of authoritarian management is appropriate to adopt even in a charity. This requires the kind of manager who tells people clearly what to do, how to do it and when to do it. The manager is then quick to discipline if there is any deviation from their orders. This style works well when there is a crisis and it would be very dangerous for any other route to be followed. It is useful when the work involves deadlines and delivery targets with, say, large problems for the beneficiaries if the tasks are not completed quickly. It is, however, a style that is alien to today's workplace and often resented by employees, so it should only be adopted when there is a real need. For some employees it is heartening to see a manager step up, take responsibility and make decisions quickly and effectively, getting everyone working together towards a common goal. Acceptance of this style often depends on the staff understanding the goal and the need for it to be met quickly and effectively. Often the manager needs to be present as this style has the drawback of taking initiative away from staff, meaning they will wait for commands before proceeding for fear of getting it wrong. It is also useful when staff may not be highly motivated but the task is imperative.

The more effective style of management in charities is the leadership style, which sets out the long-term goals of the organisation or department, and the stages (or objectives) on the path to each goal. This style means that the individual goals of staff members are aligned to the overall goals of the organisation. There will be consultation and discussion before it is time for implementation and managers will be clear that consultation has ended. This style works when the staff are professional and the manager has credibility and can persuade staff to follow her. Trust in the manager should be high and will need to be built up quite quickly, as trust comes from the validity of a manager's decisions and is not given automatically.

A slightly more democratic style may be needed before the leadership style is truly effective, assuming that there is time for team-building and building an understanding of the character of its members. This style ensures that everyone can participate in decisions and that their views are sought and respected. This works well when the team are trained professionals with experience and the tasks are within their competence. The manager is also quick to thank and praise the team when things go well. This style takes time and may not be appropriate when decisions need to be made quickly and decisively. It has been described as 'people before process' as it ensures that everyone is on board and will travel happily together before the process goes ahead.

The reverse style of 'process before people' is useful when the manager is an expert and can help staff to accomplish difficult tasks by demonstrating how they are done. This style can easily slip into micromanaging with the manager doing the work themselves. This risks the impression that the manager does not trust the staff. For managers who do not step back this can be exhausting, and is characterised by the question, "Why do I have to do everything myself?" to which the answer is, "You don't and you shouldn't." When the staff are professional and the manager can help them to master new techniques or a new process then this may be a useful but temporary style to adopt. It does set high standards and is demanding, which can be motivating for professionals.

Some managers adopt a mentoring style with their staff, helping them to achieve their goals, to develop and grow in the job or to move into a better position in the charity. This can be useful with individual staff when the manager is respected and able to encourage staff when they are keen to get on in their careers, or when the work does not need to be driven forward. In general this is not a complete management style and will fail when goal-setting is needed or staff need to be disciplined. It is, however, very useful when staff need to be motivated and a close collegiate atmosphere is required. It can settle department members into the right positions, and motivate them to develop skills and to apply for new positions within the charity (or team) when these become vacant. Sometimes a new manager will find this style useful when they are getting to know their team.

Choosing a style to fit the time and the team is important. Sometimes getting the work done is very important, and at other times it may be better to step back and work to develop relationships and the skills of the team or department. Occasionally it may even be better to use different styles with different staff members for a time, but this can be tricky as it may generate resentment or the feeling that one person is a favourite. The superhero's great attribute is the ability to be flexible and this only comes from understanding the styles, having experience of each one and learning how to apply them. A conscious choice of which style to adopt will often be required for some time, before styles are adopted automatically — leadership is not a skill we are born with, but one we can all acquire in time with experience. We may need to give ourselves this experience by trying out different styles and seeking feedback.

An air of authority

Superheroes have that air of authority, which comes from the expectation that people will listen to them, what they have to say is of interest and that people will do what they ask in the end. All this comes from two attributes – one is experience. They have authority because they have the experience that people listen to, and then feel comfortable acting on, what they say. How often have you heard weak managers speaking so hesitantly that they are almost inviting people to disagree? As a manager, merely being in a position of authority is not enough to give you an air of authority. Unfortunately however it is sometimes enough to encourage bluster and coercion, both of which traits come from the manager's personal insecurity because they cannot secure compliance from their staff.

The second attribute is knowledge. Once they know the situation thoroughly, have the right background and qualifications for the job and have confidence in a way forward then they will expect people to follow them and perform well. Before experience comes knowledge, which is the foundation on which positive experience is built. If you don't have the right knowledge then carrying out the task may not give you the positive experience that will help you in future.

We are all on this learning curve, but tackling things in the right order makes it easier and quicker to move on up the career ladder where we can have more influence and achieve significantly more positive outcomes. The shorthand for the air of authority is the way you stand, dress and speak. A superhero looks the part, is easily identifiable, well groomed and smart, appropriately dressed and talks loudly enough and clearly enough for people to hear him without straining. If he wants to he can raise his voice to cut right across the room. He is very unlikely to be silent at the back of the room; instead he is in the middle of the action where he expects to be, rather than off in the wings waiting to be approached.

The classic study of stress in the Civil Service showed that the higher someone was in the hierarchy, the more relaxed, confident and happy they were. The stress was all at the bottom of the pyramid. In the same way, superheroes become more confident and effective over time so more doors open for them. It is not good, however, to be promoted too soon and find yourself out of your depth, at which point rapidly acquiring the knowledge and skills is not at all easy and that air of authority may prove rather elusive. The reason so many top managers study on their own in the evenings, or volunteer in various roles, is precisely to acquire the knowledge and qualifications that will make them more effective and propel them forward. Each major step forward may be accompanied by a period of extra work and acquiring a new skill. This building-up of the CV is a conscious decision for specific reasons, not just whim or fancy.

Taking on new work, acquiring skills and making a difference once you are in post is hard. Jeff Bezos, founder CEO of Amazon, has said that, "A brand for a company is like a reputation for a person. You earn reputation by trying to do hard things well."

Of course, we live in a changing world and that need to prepare at each stage is rapidly being accompanied by the need to keep up with the changes that affect all our working lives.

Not only do we have to keep up with change, but once in post we have to make a difference if we are to improve the organisation and better meet the needs of our beneficiaries, and those changes often mean we are faced with taking risks. Should we use a new technology? Should we change the way we undertake this or that core task? Mark Zuckerberg, founder CEO of Facebook, believes that, "The biggest risk is not taking any risk… In a world that is changing really quickly, the only strategy that is guaranteed to fail is not taking risks."

Whilst we are thinking of quotes, I have always liked this one from Albert Einstein: "You have to learn the rules of the game, and then you have to play it better than anyone else."

That of course requires confidence in yourself, and it is no surprise that this inner confidence comes from success and it often comes early on in small but positive steps, as people engage with the world and find that they can indeed accomplish those tasks that may at first appear daunting in their youth.

Leadership and management are theoretically different, with leaders inspiring with their description of the far horizon for the organisation's aspirations. Managers on the other hand are busy maintaining, controlling and working more on systems and structures than people. In most charities the staff are knowledge workers who need to be led more than managed and who respond to inspiration more than control. If you wish to manage it is time to also become a leader, and if you wish to lead effectively it is time to emulate the superheroes, who do it so well, complete with that air of authority.

Lastly, one of the best ways of learning the skills of leadership is to observe others in action and deliberately consider what they are doing and why they are doing it. Seeing for yourself what works and what fails is an important lesson and one that is free. Look at the managers you have and think about those which you have experienced. Which of them did you enjoy working for, and which were the most successful? Were they the same? Whatever the answer – why was that?

It is not enough to have had a string of positions as a manager; many people share that experience, but how many have thought about it constructively and then tried to emulate the good and eliminate the bad things they did? Look too at the CEOs of the largest and fastest expanding companies. What makes them great? It is rarely that they just happened to be in the right place with the right idea – though that is an essential condition. Many founders, who just happened to be in the right place at the right time, were bought out and retired early as they could not retain control of their companies and didn't have what it took to grow them effectively.

Famously, Sergey Brin and Larry Page brought in Eric E Schmidt to manage Google as CEO, a professional supplying a service they didn't have the necessary experience to deliver. This was perhaps one of the all-time smart moves by a couple of geeks who knew their limitations. Eric had previously been CEO of Novell and Chief Technical Officer of Sun Microsystems so he had a very appropriate background. He could understand the people he would be working closely with and deliver to Brin and Page the very experience that they lacked. Under his management Google scaled up rapidly, opening up many new product lines and keeping innovation at the heart of the company. Eric is now the Executive Chairman.

Where does that leave the founders? According to Google's webpage, Larry Page is now the CEO (and Co-Founder) running the company operations from day to day. Sergey Brin is the Co-Founder with no other title, but directing special projects allowing him to concentrate on innovation. He has published over a dozen scientific papers.

Having observed and learnt, Larry took over as CEO, but in order to retain Eric's valuable skills he was retained in an executive capacity. Sergey can now concentrate on the area where his talents can yield the most benefit to the company; and the triumvirate was joined at one time by David C Drummond, Senior Vice-President, Corporate Development & Chief Legal Officer; Omid Kordestani, Senior Vice-President & Corporate Business Development and Ruth Porat, Senior Vice-President & Chief Financial Officer. This provided a wide skill set for the top team though some people and posts have since changed.

Facebook on the other hand is split simply in two with Mark Zuckerberg running the products side and working on growth and how the users engage with Facebook. On the other side, Cheryl Sandberg, who came from

Google, concentrates on business and bringing in the money. Surprisingly Facebook had only about twelve staff in 2005 and, though they are now in the thousands, it is not as huge as you might imagine and has survived a truly astonishing rate of growth.

Mark's management style is radically different to most. He has learnt on the job and learnt well, developing an effective style in a company of top professionals. Day one for a new hire in engineering is reputed to see six emails arrive: one detailing the usual stuff and the other five giving them jobs, such as fixing bugs, to be done and implemented on Facebook by the end of that day.

Every year to eighteen months, engineers have to change their jobs so no one gets to do the same thing over and over – zombies are just not incubated. People are hired for their talents first and then they are found a position in the company, which may seem counterintuitive, but obviously works.

Mark traditionally doesn't manage by meetings but by walking around and chatting to people. It remains to be seen how far that extends as the number of employees mushrooms. Every week, however, he runs an hour-long session answering questions from his staff. At the end of the day he is an autocratic leader and what he says goes, but it is characterised by charisma backed up by intelligence. The result is stunning success.

For the third example let's take Elon Musk's style of management. Again he is someone who built a massively successful tech-based company, or rather a series of them. First he developed Zip2 which he sold for $307m, and invested in developing PayPal, which he sold to eBay for $1.5 billion, which he then invested into Tesla Motors and later into SpaceX, which won a $1.6 billion contract with NASA. So he is doing something right.

Elon looks at what products will affect humanity, not initially at their possible profit. He then constantly invites criticism of the product so he continuously tries to improve it. Producing a brilliant product is the magic key he has found to generate huge sales, so the money goes wholly into product development, not sales. He describes himself as a 'nano-manager', going much deeper than any mere micromanager, but he also multitasks throughout the day doing several things at the same time. In this he is similar to Steve Jobs who famously distorted the reality around him by demanding and getting product developments that were seemingly impossible. Elon's style can be crushing but the very high standards he demands are exciting and life-changing to be involved in.

He takes risks, but has always has a new product get-out clause: with SpaceX, for example it was if we don't succeed with the rocket after spending $100m, we quit.

This style of management may not go down well in the third sector but I have included it to show that styles we may disapprove of will work very effectively in the right company. Superheroes come in all shapes and sizes and they can all handle the obvious human relations issues as well as the more complex ones of zombies and vampires.

11 Are you a zombie?

Are you reading this while watching afternoon television during the working week and idly thinking that the exercise machine on the shopping channel might solve a lot of your problems? If so then you are in urgent need of a check on where your life is going. It is not acceptable that no one will miss you at work. Try saying this out loud to yourself: "No one will miss me at work." How does that sound? Not good, I'll warrant.

Or if you are reading this online at work, convinced that everyone thinks you are working, it may just be that they have given up on you already. Try saying: "Everyone has given up on me." Before you despair, there are things you can do to save your soul and things the organisation should be doing to help you.

Pete's story

When the zombie blogs started, people would comment occasionally, "What's wrong with taking it easy at work, why should we slave away all day every day?" I was tempted to write a blog post called 'Zombies rising' but there is a big difference between those who may be slackers but get the work done and those who 'swing the lead' and don't get the work done or even close to it.

Pete worked for me some time back and I soon thought he wasn't much good at his job. Things took an inordinately long time to get done and even then they were not done very well. Often I would have to redo stuff or ask him to make corrections. This mattered because he was supposed to be reasonably independent, a self-starter as they say, and I had a lot of other staff to manage. Perhaps his most endearing quality was his series of silly excuses for being late to work and numerous creative reasons for not turning up at all. It was hard to tell whether he was more likely to be late or not actually make it in. Soon it became clear that he was missing sizeable chunks of the working month. Realistically, it was sizeable chunks of most working weeks.

I phoned him one day to find out just where he was and his wife answered saying he was at home, and why didn't I come round if I wanted to see him? When I retorted that he had a job to go to and I expected him to turn up to see me, she laughed. Annoyed, I said I would be there shortly and not to let him out of the house. "Fat chance of him going anywhere," she replied.

When I arrived she answered the door and pointed me towards the sitting room where Pete was watching the television and off she went to make some tea. He waved me towards a seat and started explaining the plot of the soap he was watching, as if my arrival was an everyday event and he had just invited me in to see the last in the series. While I was trying to decide if he was mentally ill and needed help, skiving or just taking a ridiculously laid-back approach to work, the programme ended, the tea arrived and Pete turned to me and asked how he could help!

Still baffled, I explained that he had the choice of improving his work or leaving. I even used the phrase "pulling his socks up," at which point he looked down and seemed puzzled to find his feet were bare. "You don't need to worry," he said, "no one is worried about me." It was his turn to look baffled as I explained I worried about him and what's more I was not going to worry about him much longer. He could either do his job properly or leave. I set out exactly what I expected from him and the timetable for improvement. He looked rather nonplussed but said, "Okay, okay," rather vaguely.

As his wife let me out I asked her if he was all right or if there was anything I should know about him. "Oh, Pete's a laugh a minute," she said which didn't help me much. I left feeling like I had entered a parallel universe full of non sequiturs and apparently lacking in consequences of any kind. It seemed that all who entered this universe lost the ability to make themselves understood.

Over the next few weeks Pete's behaviour improved slightly ahead of my desire to see the back of him but then slumped back as if the effort of turning up on time had drained his energy. He told people he was looking for another job. I had heard that before from people who were trying to avoid being fired in the hope that their manager would leave them alone and eventually forget about them. I kept the process going and eventually he was gone.

I have included Pete's story because it illustrates a situation we can find ourselves in when we become disillusioned by work. For whatever reason, we begin to slope off, then slope off a bit more, then a lot of the time and finally have trouble turning up at all. At this point you may notice that your boss doesn't seem to mind and other people around you treat it as normal. Remember Pete...

In the previous chapter we talked about superheroes but for many of us that kind of effort is out of the question. To survive at work you do not have to be a superhero (or a zombie) and you can survive quite comfortably doing good enough work, while your interests lie elsewhere or while you look for a new job. It is far easier to find a new job whilst in employment than when you have been sacked. Debilitating monotony, a tough workplace or toxic colleagues can lead to us taking time off, falling asleep in the afternoon and generally wasting our lives. This has to be met head-on; dealing with it may be much more exciting than the job itself but unless a determined effort is made, zombification sets in. Avoiding the problem by moving to another job is not necessarily a solution.

This waste is all too familiar when all we do is look forward to that dream job, or at least the next job and then the one after that, hoping that our salaries rise and we can afford to pay for the things we bought on credit last year or the year before that. We know that this is nothing to be proud of; at best we are coasting through our work hoping to land a better position at some later point all the while proclaiming our passion for the mission. If our passion for the mission were weighed against our passion for a better job I sometimes wonder which would be the greater.

Five tests to see if you are a zombie:

1. Look up – where are you? At home instead of work, midweek, feet up and bored silly?
2. Look in the mirror; see anything? Now turn the shiny side away from the wall. See anything?
3. What is the name of your boss? Does your head hurt at the thought?
4. When was the last time you completed a 'to do' list and I don't mean completed writing it: so long ago you can't remember? What's a 'to do' list?
5. Going for a new job? Been for an interview? Applied for any jobs yet? Looked online? Convinced that a headhunter will tap you on the shoulder any day now?

So how did you score? Let's just say that if you were intrigued by the survey and bothered to answer any of the questions you are probably in trouble.

Here are the times of your life when you are at your most vulnerable:

1. That first job can be a killer and establish a bad relationship between your ego and the world of work. As you probably have no relevant experience the job is likely to be boring, badly paid and involve long hours, but this is not the time to give up. Once you have this experience, however mundane, and have shown you can hack the world of work you should be soon onto your next job. In the CVs I see when interviewing, I have noticed a trail of early jobs that last two years or less, but then a stretch of three to five years which is what I am looking for. Will this person stay and get to grips with the work?

2. When you get married and have kids your ability to move home for work, put in those extra hours when required or even to study to improve your CV becomes much more limited and naturally your mind is often on your family. At that stage, it is all too easy to coast and occasionally to take time off to be with your family. If you allow that to become a routine, over time every little thing at home is much more important than work, and there you are one

day sitting on the sofa in your PJs when your boss knocks on the door.

3. You are seriously vulnerable when you didn't get that promotion and pay rise that you deserve and were quite certain you would get. You may have built that swimming pool in the back garden expecting to pay for it from the rise or perhaps you just told people you were going to build it. Then, heavy with disappointment, outrage and probably petulance, you may find that you really can't be bothered to put in any effort at work and things slide downhill slowly but steadily until rock bottom stares you in the face with a grin.

4. You become vulnerable when you achieve your dream job or the salary you chased for so many years or even the OBE that you deserve. Such achievements can leave a vacuum that only the truly ambitious never feel and for us ordinary mortals, the smell of crushed laurels can become familiar. Success and failure are not so far apart as they may seem, and one can lead to the other sometimes with embarrassing regularity. Counterintuitively, success can lead to stagnation and boredom, whilst failure can be a spur to life-changing efforts.

In Lazlo Bock's book, *Work Rules!: Insights from Inside Google that will Transform how you Live and Lead*, he writes:

"You spend more time working than doing anything else in life. It's not right that the experience should be so demotivating and dehumanising," and of course he suggests that employers should take up some of Google's excellent practices, which are great but which hinge on their attitude to their employees. They are looking for the top employees but not just to hire them and fire them. They want to retain these people and for them to grow and develop within the company. Google makes sure it gets the best of their work when they are at their most creative and primes them to excel throughout their time with the company. Naturally we cannot all have Google's profits to help us keep our staff but if we cannot equal their spending, then we can equal their attitude and use our imagination and interaction with employees to make their time at work a really worthwhile human experience.

Lazlo Bock had worked for Jack Welch, CEO and Chairman of General Electric, and observed that Jack spent 50% of his time on people matters. He built a very effective system whereby the top talent (one in five people) was challenged, moved around and encouraged. The bottom 10% were moved on if they didn't improve their performance. There was no room for people to become zombies, and managers were used to creating effective teams where everyone fully played their part.

Are you a zombie?

At Google, Lazlo saw the staff grow from some 6,000 to over 50,000. In that time it was cited five times by *Fortune* magazine as the best place to work in the US. Part of that success is that managers at Google play the role of the person on the team who clears roadblocks and makes things happen. A manager's job at Google is to inspire their team.

Google is proud of its staff policies and the ways it works to be an excellent employer, but that will not be set out here as you can easily access the information yourself, or buy the book.

Being a zombie is not an option at Google and the likelihood of their making the wrong choice in hiring is very low, as the recruitment procedure is thorough and they have a large number of applicants for every job. There is no time to sink into inactivity as the team members will just not let someone get a free ride. They are eager to succeed and to develop personally and if you combine this with hands-on managers then it is obvious that people who cannot hack it, for whatever reason, will be noticed and their problems addressed one way or the other.

In the UK we are often very poor at training managers. It is not something we believe requires training. It's as if good managers have some sort of innate skill which makes them people persons. This may be why we promote people to high office who have no experience of the management work they will do and then we compound the mistake by failing to provide management training even as an optional extra.

These managers become zombies: they do not engage with the people in their teams who are left to wallow without help in a role where they underperform indefinitely as if there were nothing to be done.

There is almost a physical precursor to zombification, which is that shudder which runs through the body when we first realise we just cannot hack this job or that we really can't be bothered to hack it. This may be followed by a lack of sleep and then the problems begin to pile up at work because we are not fully awake, though we couldn't do the job properly even if we were.

This sort of failure is not like ordinary failure of the Edison variety, where he apparently failed 10,000 times to invent the light bulb. As he said, "I have not failed. I've just found 10,000 ways that won't work." Edison's failure was the necessary precursor to success and merits praise and applause. For many of us it is an internal failure of ability or nerve that makes us question if we are up to the job and to fear being found wanting.

"Failure should be our teacher, not our undertaker. Failure is delay, not defeat. It is a temporary detour, not a dead end. Failure is something we can avoid only by saying nothing, doing nothing, and being nothing."

Denis E Waitley, US motivational speaker.

In the next section we will look at what we can do when this shudder first strikes and the consequences of taking action.

"You build on failure. You use it as a stepping stone. Close the door on the past. You don't try to forget the mistakes, but you don't dwell on it. You don't let it have any of your energy, or any of your time, or any of your space."

Johnny Cash in sombre mood.

Saving your soul

It is easy to take things much too personally, especially failure. Yet failure is a part of life and to be expected. The trick is to know how to deal with it. Moving into a job and finding that you cannot hack it, or realising that you cannot admit to the high failure rate of your tasks, are common occurrences. Recognise this and you can steel yourself to acknowledge what is happening and then you are on the road to recovery. Remember it's a road that can be taken at any stage. Tackling the problem is much harder the longer you leave it and an admission when it is still a small problem, makes it much easier to deal with. Later when things are starting to pile up as high as hollyhocks the gap between reality and expectations will seem unbridgeable.

Sometimes you may seek to be perfect and expect your work to be perfect. Then when it isn't you may feel that you are a failure in general, instead of accepting that perfection is a two-edged sword that you wield at your peril. Once you have failed it is hard to try again as you are keyed up to expect failure and your estimation of yourself falls again and so on.

Knowing that you and everyone else are going to fail, and that this failure will at times be private and at other times embarrassingly public, means that you are gaining the perspective you need to move forward and take control of your situation.

Unless you remain calm and don't overreact you will find it extremely hard to take action to deal with this kind of psychological problem, whether being calm means taking a deep breath and starting again, or talking to your manager and seeking advice or practical help. Sometimes it is easy to overreact and to blame other people or circumstances outside our control but beware of doing this automatically and lashing out immediately as it will only exacerbate the situation. At this point you need to apologise for causing the problem and perhaps also for blaming others. It is hard to do, no matter how necessary. You may have seen people dig themselves deeper and deeper into whatever hole they are in by blaming others, trying to cover up, denying it or wriggling out of it in some way. These options never end well.

You will need to cultivate resilience to the point where you can laugh at the problems that come your way, rather than denying your role, in order to keep them in perspective and allow ourselves to step back and tackle them. Listen to an interview with the Rolling Stones guitarist Keith Richards. He laughs constantly as interviewers bring up his failures, problems, gaffes and all manner of embarrassing incidents; yet he comes across as a surprisingly grounded, resilient person.

Humility is a good place to start but humility is not the same as self-pity. Admitting your mistakes or inability is the usual way out and the first person to go to is your boss. Usually that will sort the problem, but it may be that they don't much care, or don't understand the situation, and then you will need to seek advice from someone else. The driver is the desire to solve the problem, not to cover your back. Failure is one of life's great teachers and the lesson is not only about how to solve a particular problem but how to get the correct help and advice. We gain confidence when we survive a blow to our ego and sense of self-worth.

Self-pity is the other side of that particular coin, which happens to us all when we start thinking that nothing ever goes right for us, and that we are doomed to be hopeless in life. It may appear comforting but it is a false friend, as it does nothing to address the situation or to help us build up resilience and the required competences.

Instead of wallowing, staying in the present and being mindful of what is actually happening can help you to improve your situation. All this is about seeing problems as challenges and much of the advice in this area can seem like clichés, but the advice should be taken on board just enough to help you find a new pathway out of the psychological bind so typical of these situations. Being upset at a failure and feeling bad about yourself makes it that much harder to seek advice, which may mean taking another blow to your self-esteem.

After your boss the next person to talk to is your partner. This is simply a way to have a sympathetic listener and it is remarkable how much that sharing of the problem diminishes its power to hurt you. Of course, the same caveats apply and you may be worried about seeming incompetent to your partner in the same way that talking to your boss may involve a loss of face. This is precisely the problem that you must overcome as it will prompt an advance in your own development. The phrase that goes round in my head is, "Nothing matters very much and most things don't matter at all". I have no idea where it came from but it has been invaluable in putting some of my own difficulties into perspective.

However if you just let things go and potter on trying to cover up your problems, imagining that the next job (it won't be long now…) will be easier, better paid and have more respect for your abilities you may well sink stage by stage into indifference or even hostility towards your work and the organisation. Of course, you can pull yourself out of this at any time but it does get harder and harder to take that step. We are all prone to imagining that we are doing the right thing in the circumstances, until the day that we are challenged. As Mike Tyson said, "Everyone has a plan until they are punched in the face."

Regaining your soul

Regaining your soul is all about rebuilding your own inner feeling of confidence and ability. That self-confidence will come back gradually, step by step, from successes even in small things. The feeling that you can do things creates the confidence to tackle other things. You may need to put aside your grand designs for a time and concentrate on what is immediately before you.

This does not mean that you should not plan or have ambitions, but you may find these hard to hold onto when your confidence has been knocked. Start with the everyday and work in baby steps towards the next point on your journey.

The process may well start with your personal grooming. Getting your appearance up to scratch will affect the people you meet and their reaction to you will help boost your self-confidence. Once you feel down it is easy to let go of your appearance and this can have an immediate negative affect on the prospect of accomplishing anything which relies on the support of other people.

Similarly, eating well and taking regular exercise will help you feel good, improve your appearance and give you the energy you will need for the next stages of your rehabilitation.

Talk to someone who knew you when you were doing well, and let them remind you that you are capable of being successful, however limited that success may have been. Seeking advice from friends too is a good thing to do at this stage, if only because they will have an unbiased opinion about you compared to your inner voice that might be full of negativity. You can also do something about that inner voice. It doesn't have to remain negative and you should gently replace each negative thought and expression with a positive one. Realising what you are doing is the first step to correcting a poor self-image and the props required to keep it in place, but this takes work and time. Keeping at it throughout the whole recovery cycle may be necessary for a positive inner voice to become second nature.

Preventing the situation happening again helps to boost confidence. One way of working on this is to decide what you will do differently next time. When did your decline begin and what could you have done to correct the situation? There were probably several situations that became challenges, but also gave you the opportunity to change the dynamic, ask for help or plan your escape. Thinking through the past may be painful but it can also be revealing and you may need a friend whose opinion you respect to suggest what they would have done in those circumstances.

"Nothing builds self-esteem and self-confidence like accomplishment," said Thomas Carlyle.

As you begin to feel like tackling the world again, pick tasks that you feel confident you will do successfully. The idea here is to earn your own self-respect gradually and nothing succeeds in this better than concrete tasks that can be ticked off one by one. These may even be simply checking for available jobs, revising your CV, and talking to employment agencies about your next move.

Once back on your feet, a reread of the chapter on being a superhero will give you the next set of goals to work on, and avoid your story featuring at the start of a chapter in my next book. Most of us will, by definition, never be superheroes, and so long as we are up to the job we are doing can master it before too long (or move on), we are fine and should be happy with ourselves.

Back word

The observations and lessons to be learned from third sector employment and management practices also apply wherever people work, and horror stories from commercial companies appear in the media on an almost daily basis. The disappointing thing about the third sector is that it appears to be a lifestyle choice, whereby we can walk in the front door each day and feel happy and contented in jobs which may not be as rewarding financially as the commercial sector, but which are worthwhile, contribute to society and make the world a better place. All that is true but our jobs can also be riven by office politics, mismanagement and sheer incompetence, making our lives a misery as we struggle to overcome the zombies, vampires and other unsavoury creatures which lurk in our midst.

One of the Principles of Management set out in Wikiversity is equity. Under this heading it states, "Employees must be treated kindly, and justice must be enacted to ensure a just workplace. Managers should be fair and impartial when dealing with employees, giving equal attention towards all employees."

Now if that were implemented there would be no more zombies and no more vampires lurking in our organisations. It does not mean that managers should just be nice to people; rather that the enforcement of rules and of professional behaviour should be uniform across the organisation. It means that no one should be left without managerial support to achieve their best, but it also means that if staff fail to use the support provided to become competent they are likely to be fired. Setting a management competency framework makes it much easier to deal with underperforming staff.

The absolute key to an effective organisation, whether it is a charity or a for-profit organisation, is having the right people in place, performing their tasks professionally. That in turn does not mean every job requires an MBA; it is more a question of the person being suited to the work at the level they are employed.

Another of the principles is 'esprit de corps' defined as, "the need of managers to ensure and develop morale in the workplace; individually and communally. Team spirit helps develop an atmosphere of mutual trust and understanding. Team spirit helps to finish the task on time."

Unfortunately sometimes managers fail to even attempt to create esprit de corps and end up instead with something close to esprit de corpse. Management recruitment often fails at the point where interviewees are not asked about their experience of management and references are not specific enough in their questions to really ascertain if the prospective hire is a great manager or if they really have no idea. Often we recruit because the person has great experience of the charity's work, and we can see them representing the organisation with authority and a media-friendly presence, but we find out nothing about their management style or their knowledge of finance and fundraising. I have seen people appointed largely because they last worked for a top UK charity as if that meant they were perfect.

One of the trickiest aspects of management to handle effectively is the discipline of accepting authority, but balancing that with the knowledge that at times staff can, and should, go beyond the chain of command and talk to those above their immediate superior. As managers we should be able to issue instructions and expect them to be carried out, but we must also be willing to listen to other points of view or we can make serious mistakes. Failure to ensure that our instructions are carried out is a failure as a manager. It can be the start of a downward spiral as staff realise that if X didn't bother to do as instructed, they need not do so either.

Are you a zombie?

When our subordinates go to our managers to question our decisions we need to stop and consider the circumstances. Was it urgent and we were not around to deal with the problem, in which case it may not matter very much? Or is this because we have actually made a serious mistake and need to correct our approach? Or is it simply going behind our back to try and change the instruction? If it is the latter, then both managers need to put a stop to it very quickly or it will grow as a company practice.

This opens up the possibility that our own manager is weak and will just side with the staff, in which case our position is untenable and we need to change that situation or move on.

There is also the question concerning our own ability to manage a zombie boss, which may involve going above them to their superior. This is a high-risk strategy but it may be essential. It is high risk because we are dealing with someone who we will be informing that they are not doing their own job of managing their staff properly. This is one area where our emotional intelligence and social skills come into play, and is best undertaken not in the white heat of anger, but in a calm atmosphere and with constructive suggestions about how the situation may be resolved.

The last zombie

Though there are very few zombies in the third sector they clog up the smooth running of many organisations, and their cumulative effect is a drag on the whole industry. Realistically they are not a difficult problem to solve but one that does require effective management and determined action, and by the response to the blogs that started this book, that action is often sadly lacking.

Once the last zombie leaves or is brought back into productive life the whole sector will breathe a sigh of relief, and all our beneficiaries whether human, animal or planetary will be better off.

I hope that this book will speed that happy day.

Bibliography

Chapter 1 Zombies on the Board

Page 23/24   https://www.gov.uk/government/
publications/charities-and-fundraising-cc20

Chapter 2 Zombie directors and zombie staff

Page 37   http://www.computerworld.
com/article/2683239/ibm-cuts-pay-by-10-for-workers-
picked-for-training.html

Chapter 3 Hiring zombies – not

Page 61   Poundstone, W. (2012) *Are
you smart enough to work at Google*. Oxford: Oneworld
Publications, page 4.

Chapter 4 Zombie fundraising techniques

Page 87   Saffuri, N. (May 2015) *Fundraising
Magazine*. London: Civil Society Media.

Chapter 5   Zombie communications

Page 112   http://www.independent.co.uk/
voices/iv-drip/likes-dont-save-lives-unicef-campaign-
takes-on-slacktivism-8604356.html

Chapter 6   Zombie finance

Page 133   https://www.kingsfund.org.uk/
sites/files/kf/field/field_publication_file/financial-failure-
in-the-nhs-kingsfund-oct14.pdf

Page 126   https://www.economist.com/
blogs/schumpeter/2012/10/z-business-quotations

Chapter 8   Zombie charities

Page 180   http://apps.charitycommission.
gov.uk/showcharity/registerofcharities/
RegisterHomePage.aspx

Chapter 10   Enter the superhero

Page 233   https://www.brainyquote.com/
quotes/quotes/j/jeffbezos173309.html

https://www.entrepreneur.com/article/233890

http://www.virtuesforlife.com/10-great-life-lessons-from-albert-einstein/

Chapter 11 Are you a zombie

Page 245 Bok, L (2015) *Work Rules!: Insights from Inside Google that will Transform how you Live and Lead.* London: John Murray, page 8.

Page 248   http://izquotes.com/quote/191711

Page 249   http://m.imdb.com/name/nm0143599/quotes

Page 253   https://www.brainyquote.com/quotes/quotes/m/miketyson382439.html

Page 255   http://izquotes.com/quote/31839

Page 256, 257   https://en.wikiversity.org/wiki/Principles_of_Management